GW01606802

Acknowledgments.

The author wishes to thank the following for their ac[illegible]gement during the research and writing of this book: Raymond Stephens, Pat Power, Terry Doherty, Con Costello, Pat Cooke, Jim Rees, Tony O'Neill, Brian P. White, Joan Kavanagh, Dominic Martella, Veronica Skehan, Gino Forte, Robert Downes, Sean Casey, Jonathan Wheeler, Padraig Hoxey, Cameron and Chris Clotworthy, Maurice Kirwan, Mick and Marie Merrigan, Michael Kunz, Brian Harris, Al O'Donnell, Henry Cairns, Davy Donoughue, Patrick Sullivan, Jim Larner, Paul Gorry, Sean and Annie Holt, Jim Doran, Joe Dolan, Brendan Flynn, Conor O'Brien, and James Robinson. The author also wishes to acknowledge the contribution received from the Chairman and Members of Wicklow County Council, Dúchas and Wicklow Rural Partnership.

Photographs by Dominic Martella, Richard Nairn and Dúchas.

To Rory and Patsy Buckley.

Glendalough

Contents

Introduction

The Great Rebellion of 1798 was probably the most concentrated period of violence in Irish history. Tens of thousands died attempting to sever ties with Britain and to establish democratic government in Ireland. This had its roots in the French revolution of 1789 and the earlier success of American rebels which had shown the potential of radical reform to disaffected Irish Catholics and Presbyterians.

The United Irishmen were founded in late 1791 with a view to bringing persons of all religious and social backgrounds together in the quest for reform. Jointly embodied in Belfast and Dublin, they were initially a legal organization which used printed propaganda to advance their aims. United Irish Catholics, Presbyterians and Protestants (Church of Ireland) succeeded in popularising the reform agenda, but the movement was banned in May 1794 when it was realised that they had conspired with the French to overthrow the Dublin parliament.

Wolfe Tone and other leading activists were forced into exile as the United Irishmen reorganised as a secret oath bound and armed force. A sophisticated structure was developed to enhance the security of grass roots units while maintaining a chain of command with the leadership. Severe military repression in the north, however, including house burning, summary transportation and murder, badly damaged the Ulster networks in the spring of 1797. It was then that the republican mass movement made its first inroads into the provinces of Munster and Leinster. Wicklow, a traditionally peaceable and liberal county, boasted 14,000 members by early 1798. Martial Law shadowed this expansion and forced the conspirators to rise without waiting for the promised military assistance from France.

The premature outbreak of Rebellion occurred on the night of 23/24 May 1798 in the counties adjoining Dublin. Crucially, the city garrison was alerted to the threat in time to prevent an internal seizure of the capital. This ended all hope of the Rebellion being an irresistible national effort. Fighting began, nevertheless, in Wicklow, Kildare, Dublin, Carlow and Meath on the 23rd with a wave of attacks on garrison towns which quickly spread to most parts of Leinster. From 27 May the Wexfordmen made great headway after a stunning victory at Oulart Hill just as the insurgent forces elsewhere were being beaten back.

Armed with pikes and small quantities of muskets the rebels enjoyed success in rural parts of east Leinster, but lacked cannon, and found it impossible to dislodge troops from stone barracks in the larger towns. They were also hampered by mobilisation difficulties, the lack of a unified command structure and chronic munition shortages. Undeterred by heavy losses at Hacketstown, Kilcullen, Carlow, Newtownmountkennedy and Naas, the rebels took up positions in the more inaccessible mountains and bog lands around the city. The mountains of north west Wicklow gained enormous strategic importance as rebel camps were located there within easy reach of Dublin city. Wexford fell to the rebels by the last days of May 1798 but their momentum was stalled by a series of costly defeats at Newtownbarry, New Ross and Arklow between 1 June and 9 June. On 6 June the largely Presbyterian United Irishmen of Antrim and Down belatedly rose and won several minor engagements. They were prevented from forming a potentially momentous juncture with their comrades in Leinster before their defeat at Ballynahinch on 13 June.

The Dublin Castle Executive steadily regained the initiative in mid-June when large scale reinforcements arrived from Britain after which rebel held zones were isolated and defeated. The vast Irish Militia and massive yeomanry organisation raised in 1796 from loyalist civilian volunteers played a major part in the containment of the insurgent effort. The main government counterattack commenced in Wexford on 21 June at Vinegar Hill camp where a tactical error enabled the bulk of the outgunned rebels to escape into Wicklow and Kilkenny. More bitter fighting ensued, particularly in Wicklow where rebel mobility and their unfamiliar guerrilla tactics confused the military. The most effective anti-insurgent policy proved to be a liberal amnesty program introduced by Lord Cornwallis of which most rebels availed.

Several thousand militant rebels fought on in the Wicklow mountains but few were willing to persevere after a disastrous expedition into Kildare and Meath in mid-July. While dangerous to yeomen patrols and small military outposts, they were far too weak to menace the capital when the long awaited French invasion took place in Mayo on 22 August 1798. One thousand French troops under General Humbert and up to 5,000 Irish rebels won a series of victories which sparked small uprisings in hitherto inactive counties. Humbert's defeat at Ballinamuck (Longford) on 8 September, however, proved the last significant engagement of the rebellion and the secondary risings in Westmeath, Laois and Sligo soon ran out of steam.

The last vestiges of organised rebellion ended in Wicklow in November 1798 with the surrender of insurgent General Joseph Holt, although small scale resistance continued under the dynamic Michael Dwyer until December 1803. Dwyer's men harassed pro-government elements in Wicklow and embarrassed the Castle administrators who feared that continued unrest might re-interest the French in campaigning in Ireland. The sweeping powers introduced in the aftermath of Robert Emmet's plot in July 1803 led to severe repression being brought to bear in Wicklow. Coercion and amnesty quickly succeeded in pacifying the most consistently disturbed sector in Ireland from 1798 to 1803. One of the steps taken to ensure that Wicklow would never again become such a security liability was the construction of the Military Road and five barracks along its route. To this day this arterial road network provides access to some of the remotest parts of the county.

Ruán O'Donnell

Dr. Ruán O'Donnell August 1998

Planning Your Route

The Wicklow Landscape:

The Wicklow Mountains, the largest area of uplands in Ireland, dominate the county. Most of the mountains are covered by blanket bogs, on which heather and hedges grow in abundance. Many of Ireland's large rivers begin their journey here, including the Liffey, the Slaney and the Avoca. Much of the uplands form part of the Wicklow Mountains National Park which is managed by Dúchas - The Heritage Service.

To the east, west and north of the of the Mountains are lowlands, which on the eastern side run down to the coast. Sheep and cattle farming is the main agricultural activity in the lowlands along with some arable farming. Most of the urban centres are sited in the lowlands, especially along the coast, although population centres are found all over the county. There are large areas of coniferous plantation throughout Wicklow.

In the past, the upland areas were a major refuge and stronghold for those engaged in rebellion against the Crown since access to and movement across the mountains was extremely difficult for large bodies of pursuing troops. Indeed, The Military Road which runs north-south down the spine of the mountains, was built between 1800 and 1809 by the government to provide access to the mountains for troops searching for rebels.

Roads:

Today, a good road system covers the county and provides access to most of the sites listed in this book. As well as the Military Road, the N11 and the R755 run north-south down the eastern side of the mountains and the N81 passing through the west of the county. Two main roads cross the mountains from east to west, through the Sally Gap and the Wicklow Gap. In the south of the county, many roads, especially the R747, R748 and R749, provide access to historic sites.When travelling on some of the smaller roads, remember that many of them follow older routes which twist and turn sharply.

From road to site:

In the case of the urban sites, most are easily located and there is a commemorative plaque or monument in each town. For the rural sites, the maps in this book indicate the closest access point by road, from where you can make your way on foot to the site generally less than 1 kilometre away. In addition to the maps in this book, the three 1:50,000 maps, Sheets 55, 56 and 62, in the Discovery Series, produced by the Ordnance Survey of Ireland are widely available and will help you to pin-point historic sites. In the case of one or two of the more remote sites, e.g. Blackmore Hill and Luggala Mountain, proper hill-walking equipment should to be taken. This includes strong foot wear, rain gear, map and compass (and the ability to use them), whistle, food etc.

Please bear in mind, that while some of the sites are on state-owned land (this is indicated in the text), others are on private land, and you should seek the permission of the landowner before visiting the site. In all cases, however, please observe the Country Code:

- Please use stiles and gates where provided, leaving these as you found them. Avoid damaging fences and walls.
- Please take your litter away with you or deposit it in the bins where they are provided.
- Please do not light fires. Both moorlands and woodlands can be destroyed by accidental fires.
- Please keep dogs firmly under control. They can disturb sheep and frighten wildlife, and should not be brought onto the open hill which is traditional sheep farming country or onto private farm land.

Planning your Route for the day:

The historic sites shown on the accompanying map have been grouped together into six different routes;

1) Route 1, Blessington, Blackmore Hill, Athdown and Oakwood.
2) Route 2, Bray, Enniskerry, Sleamaine/Ballinvalla and Luggala.
3) Route 3, Dunlavin, Baltinglass, Derrynamuck and Leitrim.
4) Route 4, St. Kevin's Bed(Glendalough), Rathdrum, Greenan and Baravore.
5) Route 5, Newtownmountkennedy, Roundwood and Wicklow Town.
6) Route 6, Arklow, Aughrim, Tinahely, Ballyrahan Hill and Carnew.

The routes have between three and five sites located along them, so you can choose the one that will suit you for the time at your disposal, or the area most easily accessible to you. While it is best to start your trip at the town mentioned in the route name, you can of course join the route at any point. If you feel like making a longer day of it, you could join two routes together or follow a route of your own that suits your particular itinerary, visiting the sites you choose.

Remember - this is a book that reflects the Wicklow landscape. It is best used when out among the hills and valleys where rebels once made camp. So take to the hills and towns and see where it all happened!

Raymond Stephens, Dúchas.

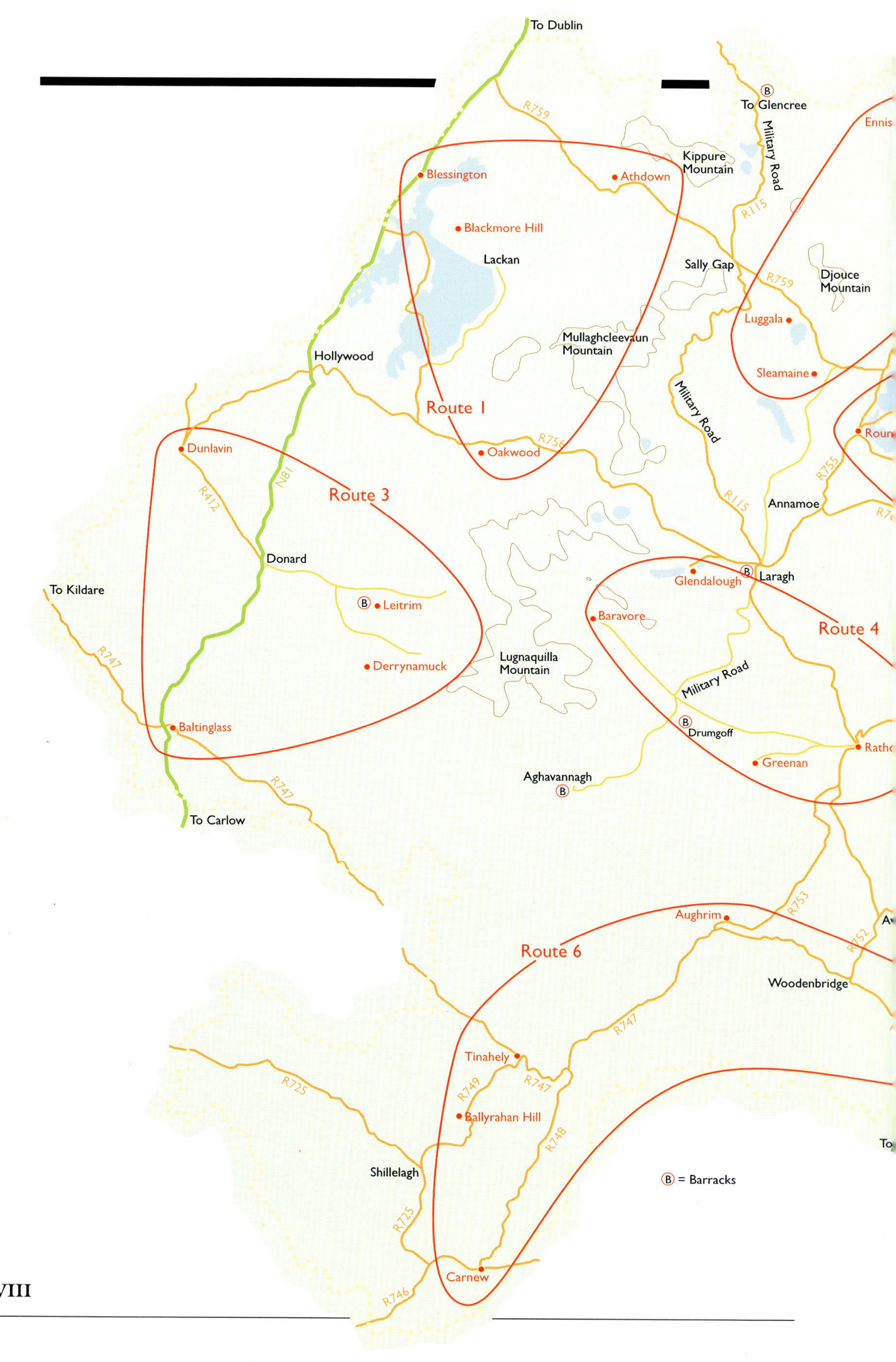
To Dublin
R759
To Glencree
Military Road
Ennis
Blessington
Athdown
Kippure Mountain
R115
Blackmore Hill
Lackan
Sally Gap
R759
Djouce Mountain
Luggala
Mullaghcleevaun Mountain
Hollywood
Sleamaine
Military Road
Route 1
Dunlavin
R756
Oakwood
N81
R412
Route 3
R755
R115
Annamoe
Donard
To Kildare
Laragh
Glendalough
Leitrim
Baravore
Route 4
R747
Derrynamuck
Lugnaquilla Mountain
Military Road
Drumgoff
Baltinglass
Greenan
Aghavannagh
R747
To Carlow
Aughrim
R753
Route 6
R752
Woodenbridge
R747
Tinahely
R725
R749
R747
Ballyrahan Hill
R748
Shillelagh
B = Barracks
R725
Carnew
R746

The routes are circled in red on the map

1) *Route One*
   Blessington
   Blackmore Hill
   Athdown
   Oakwood

2) *Route Two*
   Bray
   Enniskerry
   Sleamaine/Ballinvalla
   Luggala

3) *Route Three*
   Dunlavin
   Baltinglass
   Derrynamuck
   Leitrim

4) *Route Four*
   St. Kevin's Bed, Glendalough
   Rathdrum
   Greenan
   Baravore

5) *Route Five*
   Newtownmountkennedy
   Roundwood
   Wicklow Town

6) *Route Six*
   Arklow
   Aughrim
   Tinahely
   Ballyrahan Hill
   Carnew

Route One Blessington

Map ref. N 98 14

Main Street Blessington

History

Blessington, on the outskirts of the county near the Dublin/Kildare border, was easy prey for the rebels in 1798 owing to its proximity to their mountain bases and the weakness of local garrisons. In the last days of May 1798 raiding parties from Blackmore Hill camp burned many homes belonging to the loyalist Lower Talbotstown Cavalry which was absent on duty on the Curragh of Kildare. Major landlords suffered heavily with the biggest single loss being sustained by the absentee Marquis of Downshire. His opulent Blessington mansion was levelled and never rebuilt.

Hollywood, where pikes were first discovered in Wicklow in February 1798, was also vulnerable to the insurgents and Lord Waterford's lodge there was razed in early June 1798. The devastation appalled yeoman officer William Patrickson who in June 1798 claimed that *'few of the tenants, if any, remain to occupy the ground-all gone to the wars...Blessington is completely destroyed-not a vestige remains, except the [Protestant] church and one or two old houses occupied by papists'*. Even the church did not escape unscathed given that it was pressed into service as an auxiliary barracks by local yeomen. Holt's men occupied Blessington on 4 September 1798 within hours of its evacuation by military forces who were sent to contain the French landings in Mayo. They returned on the 5th and skirmished that night on Ballynahound Hill with the Princess of Wales' Light Dragoons.

Blessington's yeomanry were still *'under arms'* in mid-September 1801 when Lord Lieutenant Hardwicke commenced a three day grouse shooting tour of the county there. He visited Pollaphuca waterfall and Earl Milltown's residence, Russborough House, where rebels had been courtmartialled. Russborough was used as a barracks in 1798-9 by the Duke of York's Highlanders who vandalised parts of the interior to signal their displeasure at the liberal Earl's absence in Europe during the Rebellion crisis. The notorious rebel leader James Hughes was captured with two men near the house, but afterwards managed to escape from Kilmainham prison.

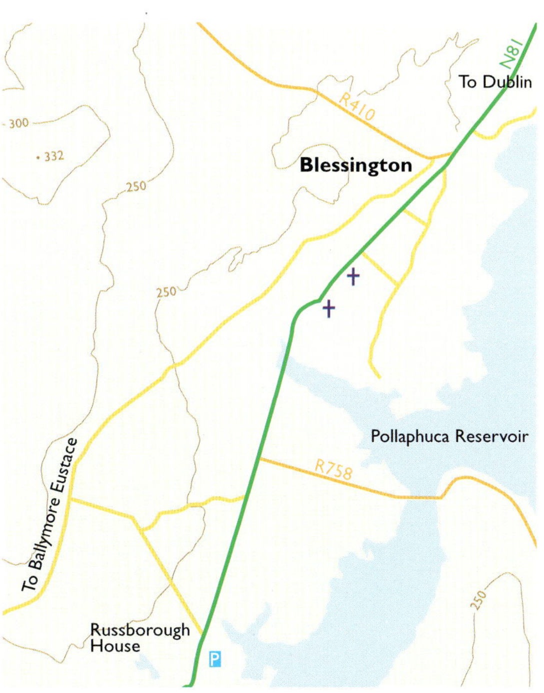

Folklore

Catholic parish priest Fr. Roger Miley informed Archbishop John Troy in June 1798 that *'for some days past we are totally convulsed both here and in the neighbouring parishes, every moral and religious sentiment has quit the country, our chapels are forsaken by the flock and nothing but anarchy, confusion, rapine, plunder and burning introduced...the cottages of the poor and the habitations of many of the middling class have shared the same fate.'*

Blessington was the headquarters of the British Peninsular War hero Major-General John Moore on several occasions in 1798. When quartered in the town on 26 July he wrote *'the weather has been so extremely bad that it has been impossible for the troops to act. Had it been favourable I should have sent detachments into the mountains, but have given them directions not to treat as enemies any parties they might see, but to endeavour to communicate with them, inform them of the proclamation [of amnesty], and offer them protection...I have endeavoured to encourage the country people by every means to come in. Above 1200 have already surrendered their arms and received 'protections', and numbers are crowding in every hour'.*

Site

Visitors to Blessington can reach the town from Dublin on the Tallaght road, the N81, which connects with the M50 ring road outside Templeogue. The L181 provides access between Blessington and Naas, the nearby county town of Kildare. While the approaches to Blessington are dominated by *'Blessington Lakes'* Reservoir this is a modern development which blocks traditional land routes to Sorrel Hill, Moanbane and other mountains from which the town was frequently raided in 1798.

Russborough House, former seat of the brewing Leeson family, is one of the best preserved big houses in Wicklow and is open to the public. Tulfarris House near Hollywood was the estate of the loyalist Hornidge family in 1798 who suffered considerable property losses.

Blackmore Hill

Blackmore Hill Map ref. O 01 12

History

In the last days of May 1798 up to 4,000 Wicklow and Kildare United Irishmen camped on Blackmore Hill where they massed their strength and prepared to take part in a proposed assault on Dublin city. The camp was founded by Kildare insurgents who had been repulsed from an attack on Naas on the night of 23 May. Wicklowmen from the northern baronies of Rathdown and Ballinacor North soon joined them from as far away as Bray and organised their men into 'companies' led by officers.

The rebels sent out foraging parties to collect livestock, food and other goods they needed to subsist and to burn the homes of their yeomen enemies. They met with little opposition as the local yeomanry unit, the Blessington Cavalry, was absent serving on the Curragh of Kildare and no troops could be spared to protect the isolated gentry homes. The Marquis of Downshire's mansion was 'burned and almost levelled' never to be rebuilt and dozens of less prominent loyalists lost their homes. Such activities put pressure on the government to act and on 31 May General Sir James Duff's 6th Dragoons and Dublin City Militia attacked the camp after bombarding it for a while with their 'battalion guns'. The rebels, however, had already determined to move deeper into the mountains and were in the process of evacuating when Duff's men arrived. Fewer than twenty were killed for no government casualties in what could easily have been a major engagement if the rebels had decided to contest the advance.

Whelp Rock, on the western slopes of Black Hill, was often used as a base of operations by Wicklow rebels and their allies from Dublin and Kildare. On 8 July 1798 a sizable rebel force departed from Whelp Rock on what proved to be futile attempt to stimulate fresh unrest in Kildare, Meath and the midlands. This ill-conceived gambit shattered the rump rebel army within days, after which General Joseph Holt and Colonel Francis McMahon of Aungier St., Dublin, were the two most senior United Irish leaders willing to fight on

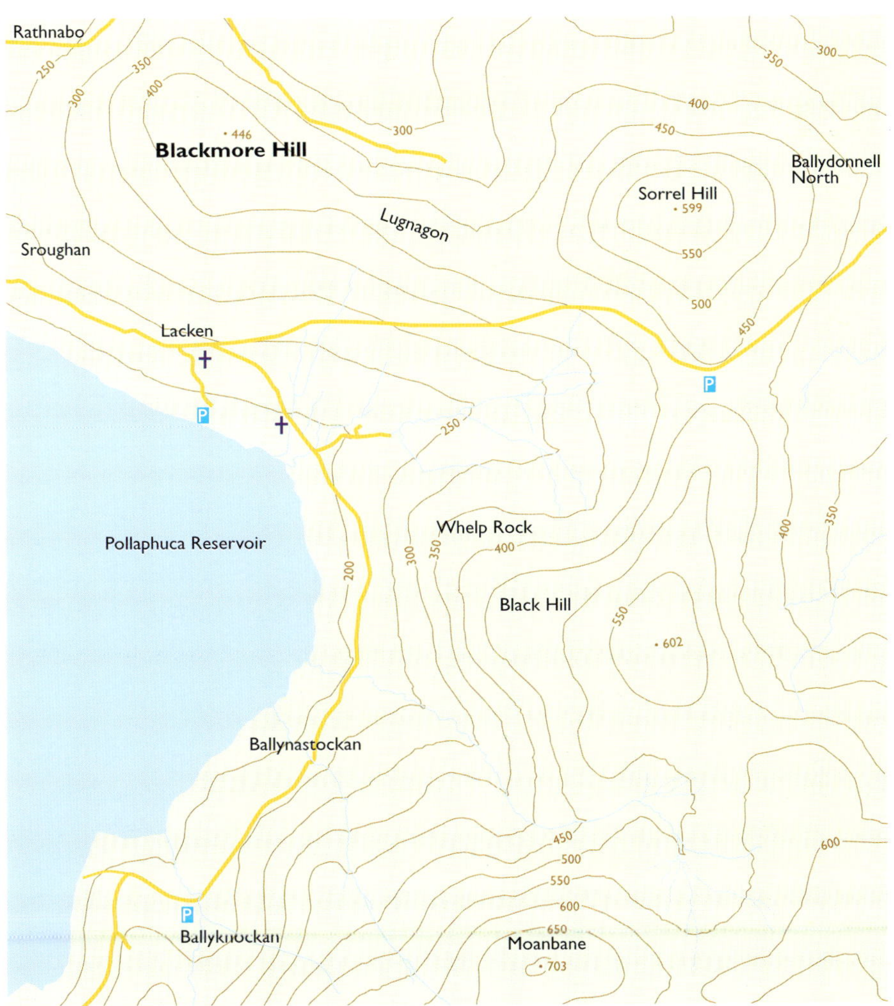

from Blackmore Hill. Crude gunpowder known as 'Holt's mixture' was manufactured by the rebels at Whelp Rock and a mounted element of the force who called themselves the 'Ballynastockan cavalry' harassed loyalists who dared to live within range of the camp until the winter of 1798.

Folklore

When cross-examined during the July 1798 trial of the ill-fated Sheares brothers, Henry and John, Captain John Warneford Armstrong of the King's County (Offaly) Militia referred to an event which had taken place during the advance on Blackmore Hill. On being questioned regarding the ill-treatment of rebel prisoners Armstrong claimed 'One was to be hanged; the other was to be flogged. We were going up Blackmore Hill under Sir James Duff; there was a party of rebels there. We met three men with green cockades; one we shot, another we hanged, and the third we flogged and made a guide of'. John Philpot Curran enquired 'Which did you make the guide of?' in answer to which Armstrong quipped: 'The one that was neither shot nor hanged'.

Site

Blackmore Hill, not to be confused with nearby Black Hill, is the ridge running west from Sorrel Hill as far as Rathnabo and Blackrock. The crest separates lands owned by the Wicklow Mountains National Park and Coillte as well as numerous townland boundaries. The western edge overlooking Pollaphouca Reservoir and Blessington, is shielded from attack by the Moanbane/Mullaghcleevaun range. This vantage offers an easy escape route into the mountains via Ballydonnell en route to Sally Gap and an alternate route towards Imaal was once available through the now partially flooded King's River Valley.

The reservoir only became a feature of the landscape in 1939 prior to which the westward view from Blackmore Hill extended across miles of west Wicklow/east Kildare lowlands. Most of the afforestation visible from the hill is also a modern development and one which would have lessened the attractiveness of the site for the ever vigilant rebels. Nearby Lackan, Sorrel Hill, Whelp Rock and the King's River Valley were also favoured rebel haunts of General Holt during the Rebellion. Holt, with the aid of Michael Dwyer, ambushed a Fermanagh Militia patrol in this area on or around 1 October 1798.

Athdown

Athdown Map ref. O 07 15

History

Athdown, a mountain townland under Seefin and adjacent to Kippure, was the scene of many incidents in the turbulent years 1798 to 1803. The rebels often passed from Oakwood and Glenbride to Ballylow and Athdown where many of their sympathisers resided. Near constant shifting of billets was necessary to keep their enemies off guard and to avoid imposing too great a burden on their harbourers. Castlekelly, moreover, on the north side of Seefingan, was the site of a rebel camp where north Wicklowmen and south county Dubliners rallied in their hundreds before moving on to the larger camp at Whelp Rock. The presence of insurgents in both camps exposed loyalist and neutral farmers to frequent raids on their livestock and assets.

In mid-July 1798 Holt, who had just escaped alone from the disastrous Meath expedition in which he was twice wounded, made his way from the city and through the Dublin mountains from Bohernabreena to Athdown. He crossed Butter Mountain and went via Scurlocksleap to the Kirwan household at Athdown before proceeding to the Kearney farm at Ballydonnell North. This was one of many sojourns by Holt in the area and in late October 1798, when he was contemplating accepting terms of surrender from Dublin Castle, the hunted rebel general returned to Athdown to pay a fleeting visit to his family. He saw his young daughter, Marianne, at Pat Mullally's house for what transpired to be the last time in fourteen years. She was subsequently placed in the care of the La Touche family of Bellvue, Delgany, until her parents returned from enforced exile in Australia.

The Brady household of Ballylow was also frequented by Holt and it was there that the Wicklowman briefed his closest followers on returning from a high level meeting of United Irishmen in Dublin city on 4 November 1798. Holt had been told that there was no prospect of immediate military assistance from France and decided to dismiss the last remnants of his much reduced and deeply fatigued rebel force. He addressed them at Ballylow before going to Powerscourt where he surrendered on the 10th. Athdown remained a noted trouble spot after Holt's capitulation and was occupied by a detachment of Duke of York's Highlanders in June 1800. This provision had been advised the previous month when a guard of fifty men was deemed sufficient to deter rebel *'outrages'* against the well affected inhabitants. The intimidating presence of the Highlanders enabled work to commence on the building of the Military Road just to the east. They shielded the project's main work camp which was then located beyond Kippure at Aurora.

Folklore

After parting from his daughter at Athdown, Holt spent the night at Ballynabrocky which he had to flee on being apprized by his host that the Powerscourt yeomanry and military were patrolling the area. He moved through the snow to Ballydonnell North, south east of Athdown, where he was sighted by a yeoman and obliged to take refuge in a river cave. He recalled: *'I leaped into this cavern and found it to be eight feet deep or thereabouts and took its course underground for some distance. I began to think what I would do as I dreaded they [had] seen me jumping into this place. I remained in this situation for a considerable time and at last put up my head and found a standing line of infantry within ten perches of me. There was a large tuft of heath growing over this place through which I put up my head and the army crossed the very place several times. I heard one of them swear "Damn his eyes but he seen me about that very place". Another said that I "dealt with the devil".'*

Site

The highest slopes of Seefin and Seefingan in Athdown are part of the Wicklow Mountains National Park. The remainder of the townland is managed by Coillte or in private ownership. With many passage tombs and barrows in its environs, it is one of the most historic parts of the county. The R759 from Kilbride passes through the lower end of the

Athdown

townland and there is parking at Kippure Bridge. The route continues to Sally Gap between Carrigvore and Tonduff North, where it meets the Military Road as it comes south from Glencree and south county Dublin. The River Liffey flows just south of Athdown and on through Ballysmuttan and Kilbride to Dublin city. In June 1802 Lord Hardwicke's administration in Dublin Castle decided against building a sixth army barracks at Liffey Head bridge, beside the source of the famous river of that name. One of the Athdown area's principal modern features, ruined Kippure House, post-dates the Rebellion, as do the woods of the Coronation Plantation which were named in honour of the ascension in 1831 of King William IV. The exposed state of the land and relatively poor quality of much of the soil hindered efforts by the Moore family and others to develop durable mountain estates.

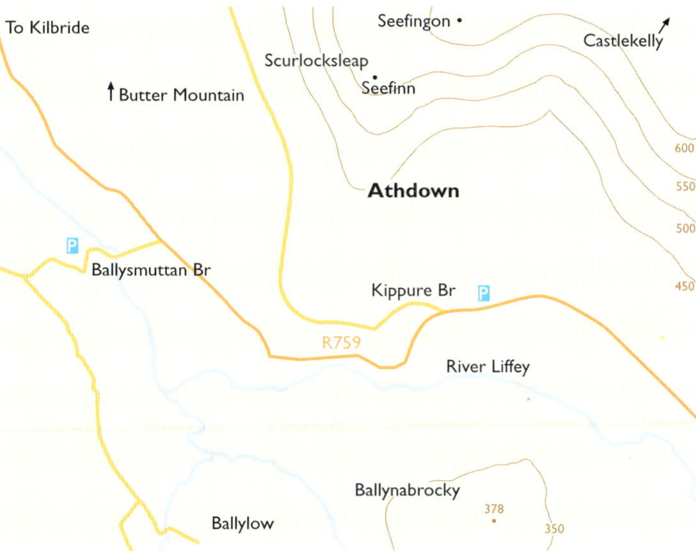

General Holt

Oakwood *Map ref.* O 03 01

History

The Oakwood district of the Kings River Valley was an extremely remote and inaccessible part of the Wicklow mountains in the 1790s and early 1800s. This, combined with its centrality, made it a common haunt of the fugitive United Irishmen in September/October 1798 and afterwards. Oakwood was within easy reach of the Wicklow Gap and the Vale of Glendasan which lay beyond, as well as Glenmalure and Seven Churches. The rebels attacked Blessington from Oakwood on 4 September 1798 and, as usual, drove off large quantities of livestock.

United Irishman Oliver Hoyle often accommodated his friend General Holt in his Knocknadroose home. Holt was there on 1 October, having just led his men out of a dangerous encirclement at Clone Hill, and planned a successful ambush of the Fermanagh Militia at Knockalt. He knew this ground very well having stayed with Widow Reilly of Knockalt and other local sympathisers. Several hundred rebels camped for a few days at a time in the Oakwood district until 10 October when they divided into smaller groups at Glenbride for tactical reasons. Glenbride was on the well trodden route to the north, straddling the strategic Billy Byrne's Gap which separates Mullaghcleevaun and Moanbane. It was also the home of the Quinns who harboured Holt and suffered grievously on this account when the military moved from Russborough House to surround their dwelling on the night of 11 October 1798. The clash claimed about twenty Irish and Scottish lives but the elusive Wicklowman escaped.

Oliver Hoyle was killed in a bloody struggle on 28 January 1801 as he violently resisted the efforts of several Seven Churches and Glenmalure rebels he had once supported to obtain supplies that he could then ill afford. This incident and the area's long term attractiveness to the insurgents added urgency to High Sheriff Thomas Archer's recommendation of May 1800 that fifty troops be stationed at Oakwood. It was in a cave at Oakwood on or around 8 December 1803 that the last remnants of the Dwyer faction decided to make terms with Government to alleviate pressure on their much persecuted harbourers.

Folklore

Holt recalled awaking from a providential dream of flames at Glenbride to find *'nine of my men lying round the fire. I roused them up and told them I had a dream that forbode to me something would happen very serious this morning. The men prepared themselves instantly for the worst. One of them went out and as he was getting over a stile at the end of the house [saw] a party of soldiers that had the house surrounded...I cried out to the remainder of my men "We are all sold. Let us now fight like men in preference to being hanged like dogs"...I then proceeded to the door and perceiving the white belt on the sargeant I shot him dead and then run out sword in hand I leaped over the dead body of the sargeant when a volley was fired at me which took the top off my hat and shot the plume I wore on it to three pieces...The army had two sargeants and four privates killed and seven wounded. Our loss was two killed, three wounded and one taken prisoner'.*

Laurence O'Keefe attended the crucial Oakwood meeting in December 1803 which brought armed resistance of the Wicklow rebels to an end and informed Luke Cullen: *'They were resolved not to draw their friends into the coils of the wolf hunter; so they drew back to the most dreary parts of the mountains...In those elevated regions the snow was very deep. There was about eight or ten of us in a cave near Wicklow Gap, not far distant from the house of one Maguire, a mountain farmer of Oakwood. None but men of the most enduring constitutions and frames could have withstood the cold and want of all the necessaries of*

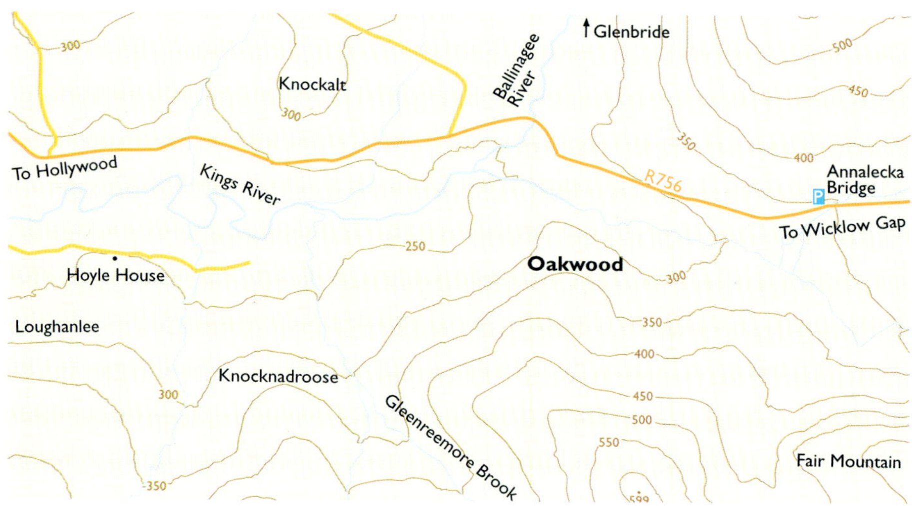

life...for every house, however poor the circumstances of the owner, had two or three soldiers...we partly came to the conclusion that we would surrender on condition of being sent to the United States of North America'.

Site

Oakwood is reached from Hollywood in west Wicklow on the R756 which passes through Wicklow Gap to Glendasan. Tree coverage on the lower slopes of Oakwood and Fair Mountain, as well as that across the valley at Garrynock and Carrignagunneen, is a comparatively recent addition to the landscape. There are few signs that Oakwood was once inhabited, but the former Hoyle house at the eastern end of nearby Knocknadroose has been rebuilt. In 1922 a republican named Neil O'Boyle was shot dead by the Free State army in the same house in which Hoyle met his end in 1801.

The Dublin Diocesan Catholic Youth Council run a hostel in the centre of Oakwood townland. Art's Cross, above Oakwood and west of Lough Firrib, is a monument to Ulster's Art O'Neil and notes the district's associations with the rebels of the Elizabethan era. No trace of the *'cave'* at Oakwood in which Dwyer's men conferred is now visible. The R756 is paralleled for several miles by a minor road on the southern side of the King's River where many of the area's current inhabitants live. There is a car park off the main road deeper into the valley at Annalecka Bridge and Glenbride is accessible by road via a spur of the Valleymount road from the R756.

Kilruddery House

Route Two

Bray Map ref. O 26 18

History

The seaside town of Bray was the location of one of the two permanent barracks in the county and had a sizable garrison of King's County (Offaly) Militia in 1798. Troops were frequently billeted in the town when on the move along the east coast. Bray was the nearest population centre to the sprawling army camp at Loughlinstown where up to five regiments formed the main reserve forces in the southeast of Ireland from 1795-1801. Many suspected United Irishmen were courtmartialled and shot in the environs of the town and dozens of others were marched from the guardhouse to Dublin to serve in the fleet.

When the Rebellion commenced extremists burned the Catholic chapel at Old Connaught, not realising that its parish priest was an ardent anti-republican. In the early 1790s Fr.

Callaghan had been pushed out to sea by French revolutionary forces and in 1798 found sanctuary in the Earl of Meath's Kilruddery mansion. Kilruddery was the base of the Bray Cavalry which carried out patrolling and escort duties during the Rebellion. Although threatened by the rebels on several occasions, Bray was never attacked.

On 30 May 1798 Lord Kingsborough of the North Cork Militia, the Dunbartonshire infantry and fifty 5th Dragoon Guards left Bray to assist in the mopping up operations after the Battle of Newtownmountkennedy. Ordered to *'make examples'* they burned the wooded south slope of the Devil's Glen in which about eighty rebels perished. The town's pro-government community and those wishing to appear as such reportedly carried arms in 1798 as they went about their business while *'the lower order, though drest [sic] in their ordinary garb, had pieces of blue or red rags prefixed to the front of their hats as badges of their loyalty'*. Not all escaped scrutiny, however, and a Bray innkeeper was arrested on 8 June 1798 for *'acting as a spy for the Anarchists of his acquaintance'*.

Folklore

In August 1798 the premier organiser of the United Irishmen, William Putnam McCabe of Belfast, visited Bray in company with his associate, James Farrell. They had returned from a secret meeting with Holt in the mountains and were drinking in Quinn's Hotel when *'a gentleman unknown to either joined the conversation, and in the course of it, stated, that he had come down to that village, for the purpose of arresting the notorious McCabe the friend of Lord Edward Fitzgerald. Both McCabe and Farrell, eagerly offered their assistance to the stranger, to attain so "desirable an object". The conversation was carried on with great spirit for some time, when the strangers separated from each other. McCabe and his friend, walked to the end of the town, ordered a post-chaise, and whilst the government messenger was on the watch, for any rebels coming from the mountains of Wicklow, they were travelling with all speed for Dublin, where both arrived, in perfect safety'.*

Site

Bray is easily reached from the capital by rail on the Dublin Area Rapid Transport (DART) line which has a major station near the sea front esplanade. It is also within reach of a number of city buses and is bypassed by the arterial N11.

The area once known as the sea common lies close to the harbour on the north side of the river. United Irishmen Tom White of Bray and Peter Burke of Long Hill (Kilmacannoge) were shot there in April 1798 as noted by a plaque unveiled on the Harbour Bar in the 1798 bicentennial year. A related plaque dedicated to three other executed rebels was unveiled that year on Kavanagh's pub in Little Bray. Another plaque honouring Luke Cullen, the pioneering Nineteenth historian from Little Bray, is affixed to the Heritage Centre in the Old Courthouse building.

The Bray associations of William Putnam McCabe were acknowledged in June 1998 when the Royal Hotel's ballroom, formerly Quinn's Hotel, was renamed in his honour. The town's liberal magistrate and yeomanry officer, Major John Edwards of Oldcourt, is remembered by a plaque in Christchurch, Church Road. Kilruddery House, substantially remodelled in 1820, is open to the public and lies just south of the town off the roundabout connecting the R761 road to Greystones with the N11 feeder road.

Enniskerry Village

Enniskerry Map ref. O 22 17

History

Enniskerry was of comparatively minor military importance in 1798 owing to the strength of the garrisons at Bray and Rathdrum. The village was, moreover, protected by its own guardhouse and by a yeomanry base on the adjacent Powerscourt estate. Lord Powerscourt, like the Earl of Meath at Kilruddery, fortified his mansion and permitted yeomen and other loyalists to live on his property during the emergency. Enniskerry was one of the first parts of Wicklow organised by the United Irishmen who may have founded a society there as early as October 1796. The charismatic influence of William Michael Byrne of Parkhill (Summerhill), Glen of the Downs, ensured that the conspiracy involved many prominent Enniskerry men. He was elected provincial delegate for the county and travelled to Cork on behalf of the Dublin based leadership.

Enniskerry's schoolmaster, Patrick Nugent, was implicated in sedition prior to the Rebellion and was shot outside Bray in April 1798 for falling out of line on the march to Dublin. Several of his comrades from the Quill, Kilmacanoge, the Glen of the Downs and Downs village itself were shot dead in the aftermath of the Battle of Newtownmountkennedy. Within days of this rampage Powerscourt yeomen captured local rebel captain Charles Gallagher of Curtlestown as he fell back from the insurgent camp on

Blackmore Hill in the north-west of the county. He was allegedly *'half strangled across a large rock of granite...then marched to Powerscourt House and without trial was shot within a few yards of the hall door'.*

Powerscourt House

It was falsely rumoured in Dublin on 24 June 1798 that 10,000 rebels had occupied Enniskerry, destroyed Powerscourt and were preparing to attack the city. Major-General William Myers led over 700 city yeomen and militia from Stephen's Green through the Scalp where they took *'every military precaution'* to avoid ambush. The column paused for a rest in Enniskerry where it was reinforced by 200 city cavalrymen and proceeded to Roundwood on what proved to be a fruitless mission. The village, however, was the venue for an important event on 10 November 1798 when General Joseph Holt, having spent the night at Bahana, surrendered himself at Powerscourt on prearranged terms of exile.

Bitterness arising from the Rebellion continued for many years and in September 1801 a yeoman was shot and wounded when guarding Powerscourt. This isolated incident did not deter Lord Lieutenant Hardwicke who visited the house in August 1802 during a tour that took him to Delgany and Newtownmountkennedy.

Folklore

A north Wicklow story has it that the local Catholic priest was shot by loyalists when attempting to dissuade the rebels from assaulting Powerscourt House in 1798. The dying clergyman allegedly *'laid a curse with his dying breath on the Powerscourt family, that no Lord P[owerscourt] should live to see his son come of age. There is a saying that no grass will grow on the spot where he was slain, and so the gravel pathway was widened to include this place'.*

The famous Patriot leader Henry Grattan purchased his Tinnehinch home outside Enniskerry in 1782 with the grant of a grateful parliament. Once in 1798 Grattan heard that *'that "the Orange boys had got up", in Wicklow, where his children were in [the] charge of their French tutor. It was not long before he found this to be true, and that the whole machinery of spies and informers was in operation about his home...the ardent loyalists of their neighbourhood were constantly complaining that no one could be found to "swear against*

Grattan"...Mrs Grattan stayed at Tinnehinch with the children, but (in April 1798) found herself threatened by the local yeomanry, one of whom turned his cattle into their orchard and garden. Finally, on hearing that the Ancient Britons (a regiment which at this period became noted for brutality) were going to raid the house, she decided to take her children to his sister's house at Blackrock; and the raiders found only servants to abuse'.

Site

The R117 provides a direct route to Enniskerry village from south Dublin through the narrow glacial valley of the Scalp. It is also accessible via the Dargle road/Powerscourt exit from the N11 which, when driving from the city, entails crossing a motorway overpass. A third road, built in the early 1800s as a spur of the Military Road, connects Enniskerry with the Glencree side of the Powerscourt estate. It meets the main body of the Military Road at the old barracks, now the Glencree Centre for Reconciliation. Enniskerry is also within range of the Dublin city buses.

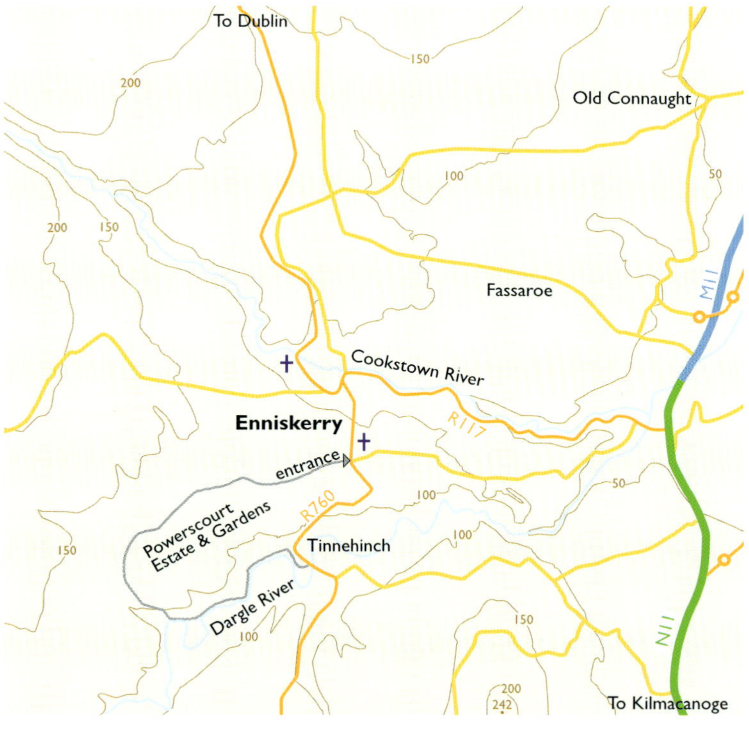

Powerscourt House and garden centre is open to the public and is located just outside Enniskerry. Although not the original eighteenth century mansion, the restored House is nevertheless a major attraction. There are, furthermore, several gentry houses in the immediate environs of Enniskerry which are of Rebellion era interest. Charleville was the seat of the Viscount Monck who was awarded a medal in 1797 for his anti-insurgent exertions with the Powerscourt Cavalry. Grattan's now ruined home at Tinnehinch was the subject of a debate in early June 1798 when British veterans of the Battle of Arklow voted by a small majority not to blow it up with their artillery.

Mullinavigue Memorial

Ballinvalla/Sleamaine Map ref. O 17 05

History

On 19 June 1798 a force of Scottish Reay Highlanders under Lieutenant McLaren and Newtownmountkennedy Cavalry under Captain Thomas Archer were spotted by the rebels on the Ballinrush side of Sleamaine, otherwise known as Ballinvalla Hill. The troops had left Roundwood and were evidently returning from a circuitous patrol which had brought them as far as Luggala Mountain when they were confronted on Sleamaine by 300 rebels under Joseph Holt. A short but intense clash occurred in which McLaren, a veteran of the Battle of Tara, claimed that twenty insurgents were killed. Holt disputed this version and insisted that the stiff resistance put up by his men had forced the military to withdraw. The insurgents crossed the mountains that night to Whelp Rock but their Annamoe associate, blacksmith Phelim Sally, was shot dead by the Newtown yeomen.

Mullinaveigue townland, below and adjoining Sleamaine to the north of Roundwood, derived its name from an old mill that once stood on the road to the village. This was Holt's home place from 1782 until 10 May 1798 when his small farm was burned by the army. He was absent and probably anticipated being denounced as a rebel leader for making an unwise overture to two Antrim militiamen billeted with him. Major Joseph Hardy of the Antrim regiment claimed that the burning of Mullinaveigue was the first such reprisal he sanctioned. Holt travelled on many occasions in 1798 from Mullinaveigue to Sleamaine and over Luggala into the comparative safety of the Wicklow mountains. The

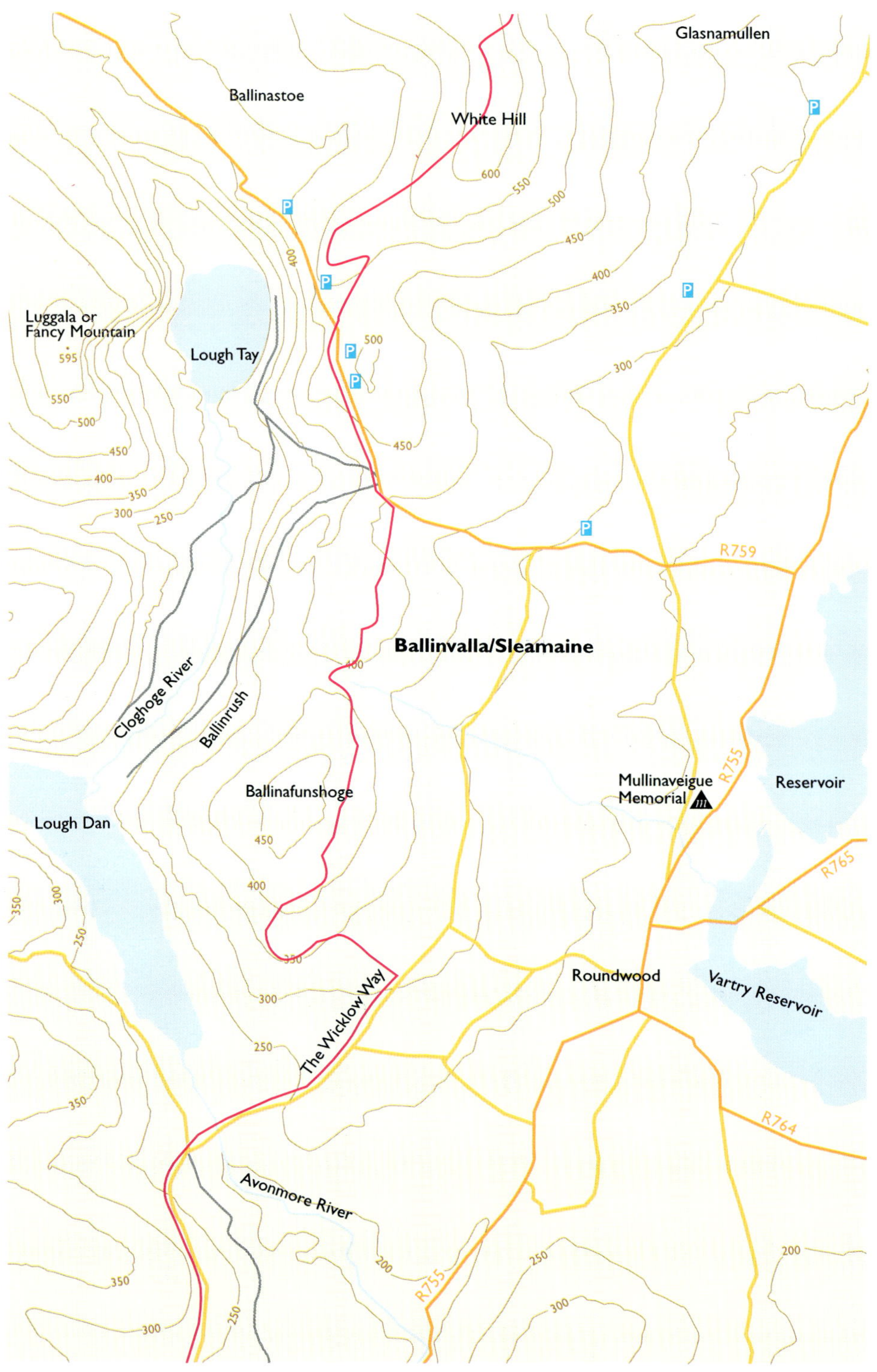
Glasnamullen
Ballinastoe
White Hill
600
550
500
450
400
350
300
Luggala or
Fancy Mountain
595
Lough Tay
500
550
500
450
400
350
300
250
450
R759
Ballinvalla/Sleamaine
400
Cloghoge River
Ballinrush
Mullinaveigue
Memorial
R755
Reservoir
Ballinafunshoge
Lough Dan
450
400
R765
350
Roundwood
Vartry Reservoir
300
The Wicklow Way
250
R764
Avonmore River
200
R755
250
200
300
350
300
250

rebel general, moreover, secreted his valuables at Mullinaveigue and narrowly avoided capture there in October 1798 when hiding in a river bank cave near to his ruined farm.

Folklore

Holt, in his idiosyncratic memoirs, recalled the Sleamaine clash as a significant occurrence. He claimed: *'We met on the side of Ballinvalla Hill. When in view of each other, both parties got quite serious. I took windward of the army and commenced quick fire. I endeavoured to force down the pikes, but to no effect. My ammunition being very scarce, I soon discovered the distance betwixt the army and me was too long to force the pikes to action which was worse of my side, having no determined person to mind the motion of the army. So, not liking the position I was in, I sent two of my best men over to the left of the part. When stationed, they began to play, or fire balls across; which threw them to confusion. I then ordered the pike men to retreat and go down the hill, as the Yeos could follow them by which means I obtained a safe retreat, tho[ugh] so few, without missing one man'.*

Site

The now wooded slopes of Sleamaine/Ballinvalla, through which the Wicklow Way is routed, had very little vegetation in 1798. The pass intervening the mountain and Ballinafunshoge, nevertheless, was important to the insurgents as it offered easy access between the favoured Cloghoge River valley to the west and the farms of the more level countryside to the east. The district was often patrolled for this reason by troops based in Roundwood and Newtownmountkennedy, typically members of the Fermanagh, Somerset and Ancient British regiments.

Few traces of Holt's Mullinaveigue farmhouse have survived but in May 1998 a large granite monument was dedicated to its former occupant on the roadside of the property. It was unveiled in the presence of many descendants from as far afield as Australia and the United States. Just north of Mullinaveigue on the R755 is Sally's Bridge which is named after the eighteenth century blacksmithing family who suffered in 1798.

Luggala - Lough Tay in snow

Luggala Map ref. O 15 07

History

Luggala Mountain, otherwise known as Fancy Mountain, is located within the picturesque but rugged heart of the Wicklow mountains. The eastern side of Luggala is skirted by the Cloghoge River valley, the water of which flows from the direction of Sally Gap down to Lough Tay and on to Lough Dan. The area was very isolated in the 1790s as it was not only roadless but poorly mapped. These factors, combined with the availability of abundant fresh water and sympathisers, enabled the rebels to mass their strength around Luggala.

Something of the remoteness of the district was captured on Jacob Neville's 1760 map of Wicklow which claimed that the area was an uninhabited *'vast tract of Mountains and Bogs'*. In the 1790s and early 1800s, however, there was a significant cluster of houses at Cloghoge where the river of that name enters Lough Dan. This valley was sheltered by Luggala Mountain and Knocknaclohogue and its inhabitants were deemed highly disaffected during the Rebellion crisis. Indeed, north Wicklow's insurgent general Joseph Holt made Cloghoge his principal base of operations in June 1798. Much of the land in the district was owned by Thomas Hugo of Drummin (Annamoe) who leased it to the High Sheriff Peter La Touche of Bellvue (Delgany) in 1798.

On 29 May 1798 the Cloghoge rebels followed Holt to attack Hugo's home, once known as *'Slaughter house'*, but were driven off by dragoons and yeomanry who rushed to the spot from another clash outside Roundwood. Hugo lost no time leading the Ancient Britons and Newtownmountkennedy Cavalry on a punitive mission to Cloghoge where all the houses were burned and many locals shot dead. This was in turn avenged on 14 June when Holt led a much larger rebel force from their camp at that place to destroy Hugo's property and that of many other loyalists. The rebels raided Roundwood from Luggala on 18 June and skirmished with a strong patrol of Reay Highlanders who came over Sleamaine/Ballinrush Hill the following day.

Ballinastoe, just north of Luggala Mountain, was inundated with over 1,000 Dublin city yeomen and troops on the night of 25 June 1798. The military expected attack from a rebel army thought to be ten times their number and passed the night uneasily near the La Touche family's Luggala Lodge at Lough Tay. The nervous soldiers were probably relieved to be recalled to the city the next day by Lord Lieutenant Cornwallis who then realised that the rebels had temporarily shifted their attentions away from the Roundwood area.

Folklore

Holt knew Thomas Hugo of Drummin very well prior to the Rebellion having subcontracted work from him to improve the Roundwood to Newtownmountkennedy road. He described Hugo as a *'cruel and inhuman tyrant. He was the first man who commenced burning houses in that part of the County Wicklow. One morning he consumed 14 of his poor tenants' houses [at Cloghoge] and came to the house of Patrick Merrigan, asking him if he had his rent. Merrigan said he would have it in the course of a week, that he had a piece of flannel and as soon as he sold he would pay him. "I shall give you a receipt in full" says Hugo, taking out a pistol and shooting him dead on the spot...this poor man was called from his bed, which prevented his disconsolate wife having the trouble of stripping him'.*

When a prisoner in Dublin Castle, Holt claimed that Owen *'Kittagh'* Byrne of Bonavally (now Ballinavalley) *'stole the beds from Luggelaw House & brought them back again at a guinea each. Owen was at the first attack on Mr. Hugo's House, but not at the burning, because he was look[e]d on as so great a Rogue to all parties, as to have sold the pass, & was trusted by no party...Owen Byrne was one of the most active men in ye Rebellion & used to stay 4 or 5 nights together in Roundwood drinking the money he rec[eive]d for pike heads'.*

Site

The mountainous crescent around Luggala extends in an apparently continuous vista from nearby Knocknaclohogue (534m) to the south around to Mullaghcleevaun East Top (795m), Duff Hill (720m), Gravale (718m) and Carrigvore (682m). The strategic pass of Sally Gap, through which the Military Road from Glencree and the R759 from Kilbride emerges, separates Carrigvore from high ground to the north that rises to Tonduff (642m), War Hill (686m) and Djouce Mountain (725m). Luggala is also just to the west of the Wicklow Way and on the opposite side of the Cloghoge River valley to the now afforested White Hill to Ballinrush segment.

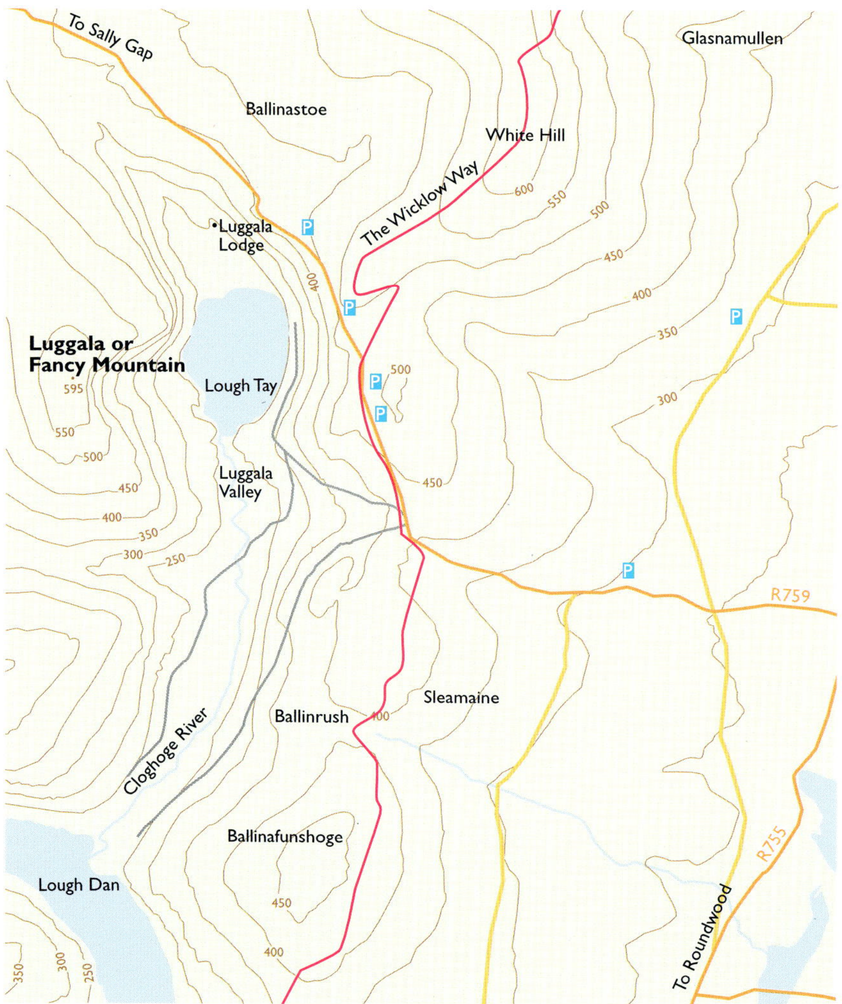

Ownership of Glendalough House in Annamoe passed from the Hugo family to the Bartons in the 1830s and was the same building in which the prominent republican Erskine Childers was arrested in November 1922. Luggala Lodge is not open to the public but is visible from the Roundwood to Sally Gap road (R579). Lough Tay's boatman in the early 1800s was Charley Carr, a former Antrim Militia grenadier, who settled in the county and was painted in 1820 by William Brocas.

Route Three
Dunlavin Map ref. N 87 01

Dunlavin Monument

History

The west Wicklow settlement of Dunlavin was the scene of one of the greatest atrocities of the 1798 Rebellion and was a known trouble spot from the winter of 1797. Suspicions as to the reliability of Catholic yeomen alarmed local loyalists who believed that the United Irishmen were very numerous in the sector. The detached Light Company of the Wicklow Militia and parties of dragoons earned a reputation for brutal conduct in the early months of 1798.

When, on 24 May 1798, news reached Dunlavin of rebel attacks on Baltinglass and Ballymore-Eustace, a decision was taken to shoot over forty untried prisoners held in the Market House. Most were indeed republicans who had infiltrated the Saundersgrove and Narraghmore yeomanries but none had been charged with acts of violence. The prisoners were flogged before being marched from their makeshift prison to the Fair Green and shot. Others had been lynched earlier that day within the confines of the Market House as part of an apparent attempt to punish and intimidate the wavering Talbotstown rebels. The dead included several senior figures in the baronial rebel organisation such as John Dwyer of Seskin and Laurence Doyle of Dunlavin.

The killings were largely the responsibility of Captain William Ryves of Rathsallagh who had survived an attempt on his life when crossing Uske Hill on 30 May. He went on to lead the Dunlavin Cavalry in many engagements of the Leinster theatre including the Battle of Vinegar Hill in June 1798. It is believed that the early success of the Rebellion in Wexford owed much to the widespread anger aroused by events in Dunlavin and Carnew.

Folklore

It is claimed that the once proud O'Toole sept of Wicklow, *'from their former prowess and brilliant associations with bygone struggles'* could not subject themselves to *'leaders of less note, such as Captain Michael Dwyer'* in 1798. Tyrlagh O'Toole of Ballymoney, reputedly a descendant of the great clan chieftains, attended one of the first meetings of the United Irishmen in west Wicklow. This took place *'on the hill over Donard for which his house was forcibly entered by the military, and all the arms and ammunition found there seized. He was also subjected to a few attacks, and some other petty annoyances, at the hands of the yeomen'.*

A vivid version of what transpired at Dunlavin Fair Green was preserved by the daughter of David Prendergast of Ballinacrow, the only survivor. It relates how *'the unfortunates were marched from the market house to the fair green, on the rising ground above the little town. In a hollow on the north side, near the gate of the Roman Catholic chapel the victims were ranged, while a platoon of the Ancient Britons stood on the high ground on the south side of the green. They fired with fatal effect on the thirty-six men. All fell-dead and dying-amid the shrieks and groans of the bystanders, among whom were their widows and relatives'.*

'Dunlavin Green', the popular ballad written shortly after the events it describes, has it that *'Michael Dwyer in the mountains to Saunders he owes a spleen, For his loyal United who were shot on Dunlavin Green'.* Captain Morley Saunders, however, was a noted moderate in 1798 and subsequently employed the grievously wounded Prendergast.

Tournant Graveyard

Site

The west Wicklow town of Dunlavin lies just off the N81 between Ballymore-Eustace and Baltinglass. The most immediate access from Dublin is off the Hollywood Crossroads onto the R756. Remarkably, Dunlavin's original Market House is extant on Main Street, as is the triangular Fair Green which divides Stephen Street and is sided by Pound and Sparrow Roads. The massacre is commemorated by a memorial erected in 1948 at the apex of the green. It is inscribed with the names of many of those who were killed.

A Wicklow '98 Committee stone was unveiled on the green on 24 May 1998. Tornant cemetery, where it is held that most of the victims were buried, adjoins Tynte Park to the south of the town but is difficult to access. Another local site of interest is Rathsallagh where Ryves once lived although the present big house is a later building.

Baltinglass Main Street

Baltinglass Map ref. S 87 89

History

Arms raiding, pike making and assassinations gave Baltinglass the reputation of being the most disaffected parish in Wicklow in the months preceding the outbreak of Rebellion. In November 1797 the baronies of Upper and Lower Talbotstown, of which Baltinglass was the main town, became the first parts of Wicklow to be placed under martial law. Up to 500 Wicklow rebels gathered outside Baltinglass on the morning of 24 May 1798 and slowly moved towards the industrial 'model' village of Stratford-on-Slaney. They were counterattacked just outside Stratford on the Baltinglass road by the small garrison of Antrim Militia, Ninth Dragoons and locally recruited yeomanry. The inexperienced and poorly armed insurgents expected little resistance from the military and when challenged withdrew towards Baltinglass. They were pressured by the dragoons who routed them when the Baltinglass Cavalry led by Captain Benjamin O'Neil Stratford sealed off their avenue of retreat. Twenty pro-government forces were wounded but none killed in return for dozens of rebel fatalities.

During the clash, Thomas Kavanagh, a leading United Irishman in Talbotstown, defected to the rebels from the Baltinglass Cavalry. Forced to flee when matters turned for the worse, he was betrayed and arrested later that day at Manger in the home of William and Rachael Valentine. Kavanagh was promptly executed in Baltinglass and his skull was still spiked on the roof the town's guardhouse on 10 February 1799 when rebels attached to James Hughes' faction avenged him by killing Mrs Valentine and burning her home.

The proximity of Baltinglass to the Glen of Imaal ensured that it remained a place of note in the aftermath of 1798 and the centre of operations against the Dwyer group until 1803. On 8 December 1798 five yeomen and soldiers were killed on the old Shruhaun road that ran between Eldon Bridge and the town on the eastern side of the River Slaney. Many of Dwyer's closest companions were ultimately executed in Baltinglass and virtually all his extended family were detained there in October/November 1803 prior to their transferral to Dublin prisons.

There was another sizable yeomanry base about seven kilometres to the south of Baltinglass at Humewood, near Kiltegan. Humewood was the home of liberal MP William Hume who was killed when skirmishing with mounted rebels on 8 October 1798 at the base of Keadeen Mountain. His parliamentary seat and captaincy of the Upper Talbotstown Cavalry devolved on his son, William Hoare Hume, who had distinguished himself during the Rebellion. Dwyer entered negotiations with Hoare Hume in late 1803 and, when all the arrangements were in place, surrendered to him at the gates of the estate on 14 December 1803.

Dwyer/McAllister Memorial

Folklore

Martin Burke of Donaghmore, Dwyer's right hand man, was caught off guard at Leitrim (Imaal) in September 1798 and taken to Baltinglass prison: *'Since the battle of Stratford this den or hell of the Hon. Benjamin O'Neil Stratford, was crowded to suffocation with the bravest spirits of that country. From the great number confined there and the total absence of all regard to cleanliness or decency it had become an intolerable sink of filth...One night there was plenty of the ardent stuff going round; the guards became drowsy, and Burke stretched on a form, with one hand fastened to his side, pretended to sleep. He watched his best opportunity, and, rising, went to the man who had the key, and, on a point of decency, begged him to go outside the door with him. The guardsman unlocked the door and accompanied his prisoner. They had no sooner gone into the yard than Burke turned on him and felled him with a tremendous blow. He lost no time in crossing the river near the old Abbey; concealed himself there, and sent for a smith to take off his irons'.*

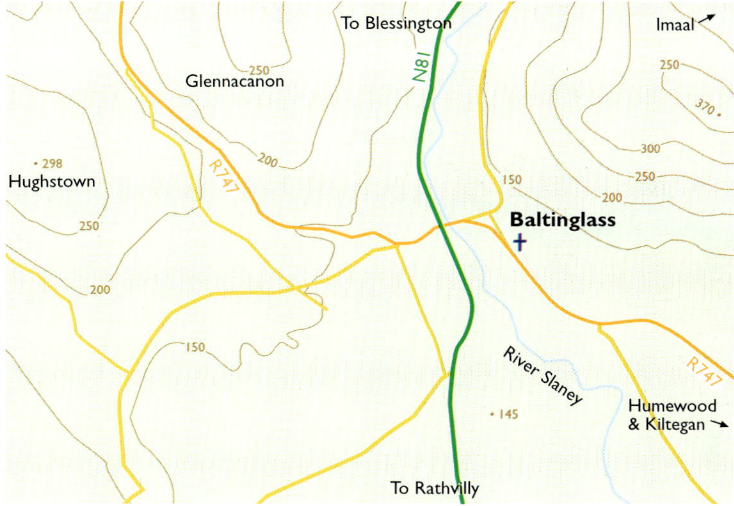

Burke was recaptured by the Monaghan Militia at Stranahely on 10 December 1803 when, owing to negotiations aimed at securing the surrender of the whole Dwyer faction, he was permitted to exile himself with them in Australia.

Site

The principal route to Baltinglass from Dublin is the N81 which continues to Tullow in Carlow. Baltinglass sustained little damage in 1798 and was never threatened after 24 May 1798. The *'Dwyer-McAllister'* memorial is the town's main commemorative structure and was built in May 1904 using a nucleus of funds left over from the county town's 'Billy Byrne' monument. It is dedicated to the victims of the Derrynamuck ambush of February 1799. A more general memorial was unveiled on 8 August 1998 at Gillespie's shop, the site of Baltinglass Courthouse and Prison in the 1790s.

Saundersgrove House and the ruined Stratford Lodge, properties which belonged to Captain Morley Saunders and the politically divided Stratford family in 1798, are both just north of Baltinglass. The townland of Talbotstown, from where Thomas Kavanagh hailed, is a few kilometres south east of the town but there are few parts of the surrounding district that are not steeped in the history and lore of the Wicklow Rebellion. One of the most significant historic buildings, Humewood Castle, still stands on the Kiltegan estate although its connection with the Humes ended in the early 1990s.

Vicinity of Michael Dwyer Cottage

Derrynamuck Map ref. S 96 91

History

The townland of Derrynamuck, Donaghmore parish, lies under Keadeen Mountain in the rugged Glen of Imaal of west Wicklow. This area, more than any other in the county, is associated with the exploits and adventures of Michael Dwyer and his followers between 1798 and 1803. Having fought with the Wicklow and Wexford insurgents from May to October 1798, Dwyer and a small group of battle hardened insurgents returned to their native Imaal where they remained on the run for most of the next five years.

Derrynamuck became the scene of the greatest reverse suffered by Imaal rebels in the Rebellion period on 15 February 1799. Dwyer and twelve men took shelter from a snowstorm in three houses in which they had often been harboured before. On this occasion, however, news of their presence was conveyed to the garrison of Hacketstown causing a strong force of Glengary Highlanders to rush to the spot. All the rebels surrendered apart from the three men billeted with Dwyer in Miley Connell's cottage, who mounted what they must have presumed was a *'last stand'*.

The terrific volume of fire poured into Connell's soon killed John Savage and Patrick Costello and smashed the arm of Antrim Militia defector Samuel McAllister. This evidently suggested a famous ruse to McAllister in which he deliberately drew the fire of the soldiers to give Dwyer a chance to escape. Incredibly, the northerner's sacrifice achieved its object and the Imaal leader caught his enemies off guard as he fled into the night. He crossed the Little Slaney River and ran to Colliga where he procured a horse from a yeoman sympathiser which bore him to safety at Knockgorragh.

Eight of those taken prisoner at Derrynamuck were sentenced to death in Baltinglass and all but one, who turned informer, were executed within the week. This delivered a heavy blow to Dwyer but steeled him to tighten his security precautions and to take a harder attitude towards suspected informers. Dwyer continued to frequent Derrynamuck, however, and was drying gunpowder in the adjacent townland of Rostyduff in July 1803 when news reached him of the premature rising of Robert Emmet. The Wicklowman had twice conferred with Emmet in south Dublin and on learning of the debacle in the city sent word to him that he would 'rise' if requested to do so.

Folklore

Dwyer/McAllister Cottage

William Hanbidge of Tinnehinch, Imaal, remembered a story of how his father rejected an offer by a friend, Tom Hayden, to join the United Irishmen in late 1797. The next day Hayden *'came and asked for the repayment of some money which he had lent him. Later in the spring of 1798 Hayden strove to persuade my father to give over planting potatoes saying that no one would ever dig them. The Haydens was quite a harmless family but evidently knew all about the conspiracy. When the outbreak took place they often saved my fathers' house from being burnt...Dwyer became a captain among them and was not at all bloodthirsty for many of the lives of the Co. Wicklow Protestants he saved...in 1798 practically every small Protestant farmer in the Glen was enroled in the Yeomanry'.*

An 1858 version of the Derrynamuck story asserts that *'As Dwyer saw no alternative, but to be buried alive or submit to the enemy, he agreed to the proposal of McAl[l]ister, and having tenderly embraced each other, McAl[l]ister and [John] Savage advanced to the door, dashed it open, and ran out; they were instantly shot down and in the twinkling of an eye Dwyer bounded out through the midst of the soldiers, leaped a small fence, that surrounded the farmyard, and ran along by the door of the barn, but in passing a small stream, that was frozen, which ran by the end of the cabbage garden, his foot slipt on the ice, and he fell flat on*

his face. To this fall he most miraculously owed the preservation of his life, and his final escape, for he had scarcely reached the ground, when a score of balls, fired by the Highlanders at him, passed harmlessly over his head'.

Site

The Derrynamuck area of Imaal remains unspoilt and is well sign posted owing to public interest in the restored cottage. The Dwyer-McAllister cottage, was opened in August 1948 by President Sean T. O'Ceallaigh and visiting details are posted up all year round. The building is owned and managed by Dúchas, The Heritage Service.

Much of what attracted the Dwyer group to the district is apparent today, not least that Derrynamuck is overlooked on three sides by difficult mountainous terrain. Guard posts at Davidstown to the east and Rathdangan to the south did not impinge on the traverses of the rebels through the nearby Ballinabarny gap. Derrynamuck is also very close to the foot paths across the highlands spanning Table Mountain (701 metres) to Lugnaquillia (925 metres) which seals the eastern extremity of Imaal and divides the valley from Glenmalure. Today the army's Glen of Imaal Artillery Range blocks traditional walking routes that were much in use during the Rebellion years.

Ruins of Leitrim Barracks

Leitrim Map ref. S 97 94

History

Leitrim, in the Glen of Imaal, is primarily recalled as the site of one of the five substantial barracks built along or near the Military Road in the aftermath of 1798 in Wicklow. In April 1798 an army camp was formed at nearby Knockanarrigan but that location was not deemed suitable for a permanent barracks. Leitrim was probably favoured by the Royal Irish Engineer surveyors owing to its proximity to the terminus of the Military Road which was completed in 1809.

The brutality displayed by the soldiers at Knockanariggan in 1798, and in particular their practice of conscripting unpaid local labour, complicated the building of Leitrim when work commenced in the spring of 1803. The barracks project provided the outstanding Imaal rebels with access to gunpowder donated by workers who often left them gifts of whiskey. It is said that *'Captain Dwyer...from the day of his first taking the field to his surrender, scarcely ever fired a charge of powder that did not come out of His Majesty's stores'.* In June 1803 Dwyer conversed with a military work detail as they blasted stones for the barracks from a quarry near Leitrim. The building was finished in 1805 but local tranquillity and changes in strategic thinking ensured that it was never occupied by the 200 men it was designed to house.

Leitrim

Antrim Militia defectors Samuel McAllister and Adam Magee were buried in Leitrim cemetery in February 1799 but quickly moved to a more suitable resting place by women rebel sympathisers. Ann Devlin was one of those who assisted and recalled *'the wind blew such a furious gale that we were obliged to secure the coffins, they being very light, from being blown away. We soon stripped the bodies of their earthly shrouding. They had been interred with a quantity of hay around them. We succeeded in taking up all together and placed them in the coffins and proceeded to Kilranalagh, where the grave was open to receive them...we knelt down and prayed for the souls of the young men, not excluding the noble spirit of McAl[l]ister, who was a Presbyterian'.*

Folklore

In mid-June 1803 Glenmalure rebel John Mernagh and Laurence O'Keefe found themselves trapped by the military for forty hours in an underground bunker at Leitrim. *'When night drew its veil along the dark Glen of Imaal, they loaded all their arms and went straight to the barrack, the walls of which had now reached the elevation of twenty five or thirty feet. They soon found some crowbars and then set to with the greatest diligence and expedition to throw down the mason work, and in a short time (says O'Keeffe) an immense quantity of the work was cast down... It was positively affirmed that there should have been several hundred men engaged in that diabolical destruction of that splendid homestead that was rapidly advancing to completion to domicile the journeymen butchers of their fellowmen'.*

Another story has it that there was a subterranean hide at Leitrim known only to Dwyer and Samuel McAllister in which the sleeping Imaal insurgent was awakened by a vision of his dead comrade. Dwyer heeded the warning to leave the dugout and had just done so when it was discovered by the military.

Site

Leitrim is located in the far reaches of Imaal and accessed by road from Dublin via Blessington and Donard. One may also drive the length of the valley through Donaghmore to Knockanariggan and out to Leitrim via Bushfield. Very little of Leitrim barracks remains to be seen and the best preserved part of the ruin is thought to be a later guardhouse addition.

Camara, where Michael Dwyer was born in 1772, lies only 2 kilometres south-east of Leitrim but within the Glen Imaal Artillery Range and is not generally open to the public. Details may be obtained from the Army Information and Advice Centre. The townland of Seskin, however, is just across the River Slaney from Leitrim and is of interest as the home of Dwyer's uncle John, a United Irish baronial delegate for Talbotstown who was shot at Dunlavin. It is also the place to which the bodies of McAllister and Magee were brought prior to their reburial in Kilranalagh. When Michael Dwyer first took to the field in May 1798 he ascended the familiar ground of Lugnaquillia Mountain and from that moment used his intimate knowledge of Imaal geography to keep one step ahead of his enemies for five years.

St. Kevins Bed

Route Four
St. Kevin's Bed (Glendalough) Map ref. T 10 96

History
Possession of the historic Vale of Glendalough, known as the Seven Churches in the eighteenth century, constantly alternated between rebels and government forces in 1798. Small bands of rebels continued to frequent Seven Churches in the aftermath of 1798 to take advantage of the district's many caves and lead mine shafts in which they could hide and store goods. A major build up of insurgent forces occurred in Glendasan on 17 June 1798 during which a number of loyalist prisoners were escorted to Glendalough for safe keeping. The fighting elements under General Holt re-entered the valley the following week where, for the first time in the Rebellion, his north Wicklowmen joined forces with their comrades in the Ballymanus Division who had just escaped from Vinegar Hill in Wexford. Garret Byrne's men were accompanied by hundreds, if not thousands, of north Wexfordmen, some of whom insisted that at least ten captives be tried to ascertain if they were *'orangemen'*.

One of those tried on the 23rd was the Synge family's wood ranger, Joseph Thompson of Roundwood, who claimed that they were *'kept prisoners in an old yard [and] when the Wexford rebels join[e]d those of the county of Wicklow...driven down by a mob of the rebels to the butt of the steeple'* to be piked. Friends and neighbours of the prisoners objected to the proposed executions whereupon *'some of them so far interfered on their behalf to the officers that at last their lives were spared on condition of their joining the rebels, w[hi]ch they did, till they had an opportunity of escaping'.*

The rebel army then numbered several thousands and left Seven Churches on the morning of 24 June to climb into Glenmalure en route to Hacketstown which they attacked and destroyed on the 25th. Glendalough was flooded with troops in mid-July, who converged on the valley from several directions to force the rebels to a battle they could not win. Major-General Moore's column descended from Table Mountain, but failed to trap the elusive rebels either then or in a repeat of the operation the following month.

St. Kevin's Bed, in the cliffs over the southern end of the Upper Lake of Glendalough on the Lugduff side, is associated with several incidents in the Rebellion years. Most concern Michael Dwyer and his faction, who enjoyed very close links with the Seven Churches insurgents. In December 1800 a captured member of the group was pressurised into revealing the location of an important hide near St. Kevin's Bed. A military patrol found a hastily evacuated cave stocked with bedding for several men, dried provisions, casks of drink and the carcasses of six recently slaughtered sheep. It was partly to deter such activities that Laragh, on the eastern approaches to Glendalough, was selected as a site of an army barracks built along the Military Road between 1803 and 1807.

Folklore

One of the earliest stories linking Dwyer to St. Kevin's Bed claims that he was *'one summer's morning lying fast asleep in the bed, and a serjeant's guard of the Highlanders was patrolling along the other side of the lake..the party was commanded by serjeant Donald McBane...one of the best shots that ever rammed down a bullet; some people were even led to believe he could shoot a man round a corner. Well-this canny Sawney, thought he saw something in the bed, and he ups with his terrible gun, and sure enough he was near giving Dwyer his billet for the other world-for the ball grazed his thigh, cut away the skin upon his ribs, but did no real injury…naked that he might run light, he took to his well known pass up the face of Lugduff. The Highlanders, like sporting fellows, immediately grounded their muskets, and, bayonet in hand, started off in pursuit: some making after him by the head of the lake, towards Gleneola [River]; others turned to the left, and made their way over the stream by Pol[l]anass'.*

On glancing over his shoulder Dwyer noticed the awkward dispositions of the soldiers and changed his plan. He allegedly ran back down Lugduff, *'plunged into the lake at Templenaskellig, swam across the water before you could say Jack Robinson, and took possession of the Scotchmen's muskets and cartridge boxes...one after another he pitched the guns and ammunition into the lake; you could hear his huzzas rattling and echoing through the hills…he then very leisurely lounged away towards Toulenagee mountain, and so off towards his old haunts under Lugnaquill[i]a'.*

Site

Glendalough, one of Ireland's premier tourist locations, is well sign posted and provided for by a Visitors' Centre. It is within easy reach of the N11 via Ashford and Annamoe and from Rathdrum on the R755. The Military Road from Sally Gap enters nearby Laragh while the R756 provides access from Hollywood in the west of the county. The Wicklow Way passes over Paddock Hill and around Derrybawn before rising over Mullacor to Glenmalure. The rebels favoured Glendalough as it offered them the valuble options of a quick escape through Glendasan and Wicklow Gap into the King's River Valley or across Mullacor/Lugduff mountains into Glenmalure.

Photo: Dúchas
St. Kevins Bed

St. Kevin's Bed is a man made opening cut into the face of the cliffs near Templenaskellig about twenty feet over the Upper Lake. It is approximately two metres deep and one in diameter and is thought to have been a bronze age burial site. The Bed is inaccessible and would otherwise have been of little value to the Wicklow insurgents. No other rock shelter, cave or mine in Glendalough can be positively identified with the United Irishmen but there is a strong tradition that *'Dwyer's Bed'* or *'Dwyer's Rock'* on the southern slope of Camaderry, near the lower portion of the Upper Lake, was used by the Imaal man. Laragh barracks was used by the Royal Irish Constabulary from 1830 until the early 1920s when it was badly damaged by republicans. Although altered when rebuilt as a private residence, the original materials were reused and both the arch gateway and outer wall are untouched.

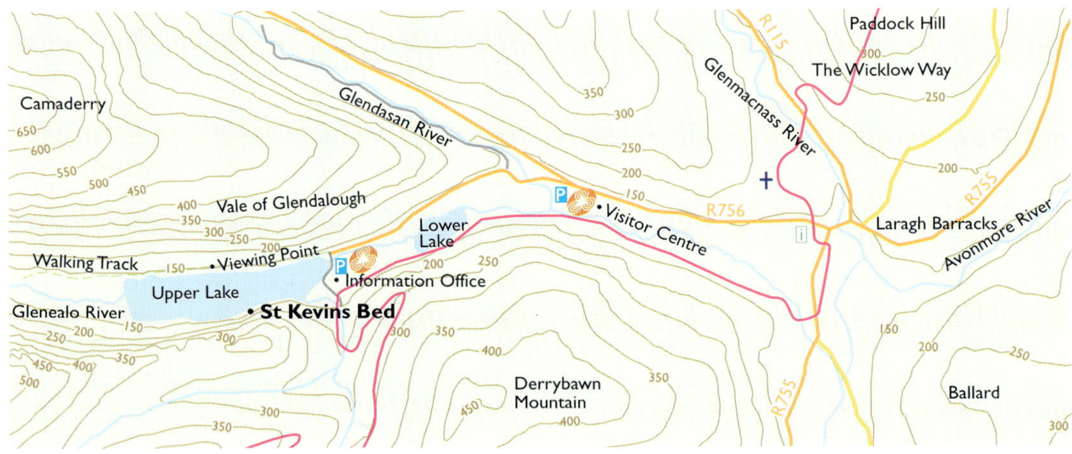

Rathdrum Map ref. T 18 88

History

The mountain market town of Rathdrum, after Arklow, was the most strategic settlement in the county. Yeomen based here included ninety Cronebane miners enlisted in the Rathdrum infantry who sallied out to Ballinvally gold mine on 31 May 1798. They collected materials used in converting the Flannel Hall into a barracks which, along with a government grant of £500, transformed that spacious building into a *'fort'* capable of accommodating 450 troops.

Universal Flame Monument

The town's yeomanry captured a key rebel emissary at Cronebane on 11 June who, when courtmartialled in Rathdrum, admitted having travelled throughout the mountains to co-ordinate rebel attacks on behalf of the Dublin leadership. In late June 1798 Rathdrum was garrisoned by about 300 Dublin City Militia and Reay Highlanders with a three pounder cannon. Troop numbers swelled to some 1,400 in mid-July when the Marquis of Huntley, son of the Duke of Gordon, billeted soldiers being used in the campaign against Holt's rebels in Glenmalure. On 12 July 1798 a young army officer hoped that Huntley would join Rev. Powell and Rathdrum's masonic 'friendly brothers' in their annual dinner in Bates' Inn.

Although too strong a post to be vulnerable to the rebels, Michael Dwyer's men attacked yeomanry homes on the outskirts of Rathdrum on 16 October 1798. Loyalists at Ballinderry, Ballyteigue and Corballis lost their homes as the bulk of the garrison were absent searching for Holt in Oakwood. The raid was intended to avenge the murder of a pardoned Killincarrig rebel whose acquittal owed much to the testimony of Rathdrum loyalists.

Captain Thomas King of Kingston was Rathdrum's principal magistrate and the most committed opponent of the Dwyer group. King was an early advocate of the hard line anti-insurgent tactics and legal measures which ultimately proved successful in containing the Wicklow rebels. Under King's auspices dozens of captured United Irishmen were courtmartialled in the Flannel Hall between 1798 and 1801, some of whom were prosecuted by the infamous 'Croppy Biddy' Dolan. An unknown number of those capitally convicted were shot and buried on the adjacent Fair Green.

Folklore

Wicklow heroine Ann Devlin lived with her family at Corballis when Dwyer's men struck in October 1798. She recalled meeting *'Dwyer and the rest of my cousins and the whole party as they marched away from Manning's house after burning it. In a few minutes we were at my uncle's house and the whole family set to prepare refreshments for the visitors. Dwyer and his thirty men billeted themselves that night within two and a half miles of Rathdrum'.*

One of those shot on the Fair Green in 1799 was the popular United Irishman Terence 'Kittagh' Byrne of Bonavalley. Luke Cullen ascertained that *'about the same time a batch of men were brought up to the Fair green..and shot. One of them, named (James) Murphy either from Ballycullen or Agho[w]le...was ordered with a stern and peremptory voice to kneel down. On such occasions the loyalists all thought they had a right to command, and several voices cried out, "Kneel down on your coffin". He gave a look of indignation around him, leaped on the slight shell and drove the lid down to the bottom, and firmly stood for their fire'.*

Site

Rathdrum is reached from the north by the R755 from Laragh and the R752 from Glenealy which intersect outside the town. It is said that the road skirting Rathdrum towards Avondale was built in response to a Rebellion era incident in which horses collapsed when pulling cannon up the steep main road into the town and had to be cut free from their load.

Rathdrum has grown into a large town since the Rebellion years but retains many features of that tragic period. The Cartoon Inn on the village square was formerly Bates' Inn where Volunteer, masonic, yeomanry and Orange Order meetings took place in the 1790s and early 1800s. There is a memorial dedicated by Thomas King in the Church of Ireland and his fortified seventeenth century home, Kingston, stands close to Avondale. While Avondale is principally remembered as the home of nationalist parliamentarian Charles Stewart Parnell it was the estate of his conservative ancestor Sir John Parnell in 1798.

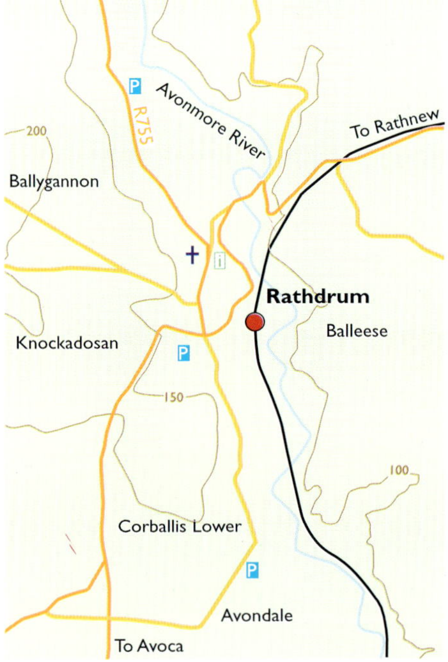

Portions of brickwork belonging to what was once the extensive Flannel Hall can be seen at the base of the building cluster which fronts the lower end of the Fair Green. The Hall was built by Earl Fitzwilliam in 1795 to encourage the booming cloth trade and was so useful to the army that he experienced great difficulty recovering it from the Barrack Board in 1801. The United Irishmen of Rathdrum are commemorated on the Fair Green by a memorial garden created in 1998, complete with a fine monument.

Lower Glenmalure

Greenan (Lower Glenmalure) Map ref. T 14 87

History

The lower end of the Glenmalure valley was the conduit for numerous attacks on and by the rebel forces in 1798. The strong garrison at Rathdrum proved incapable of preventing insurgent utilisation of Glenmalure as one of their principal camping grounds during the summer months. Greenan, at the mouth of Glenmalure, was then the main settlement in the area and contained a thriving cloth printing factory owned by Henry Allen. This changed at the onset of the Rebellion when the labour supply was disrupted and came to a permanent halt in late July 1798 when Holt's men burned it to the ground to prevent its conversion into an auxiliary barracks. Many of those who played an active role in the attack were thrown out of work. Suspected *'orangeman'* John Wheeler and his son Samuel were killed during the raid and had their bodies thrown into the Avonbeg River from Greenan Bridge. The inevitable revenge attacks by loyalists claimed many local properties and a number of lives.

Ballinacor townland, under the mountain which bears its name, was the home place of James Doyle who was one of the most effective insurgent captains in the Ballymanus Division. Michael Dwyer, whose aunt lived at Carriglineen, fought in the Glenmalure company of rebels led by Doyle in Wexford in June 1798. Ballintombay, on the opposite side of the Avonbeg River, was home to Michael Malone who resigned his captaincy in the

Glenmalure Memorial

insurgent forces to protest the decision to execute loyalist prisoners at The Strand. Most of those piked were members of the Rathdrum yeomanry who were held responsible for atrocities before and during the Rebellion. Rebel victims in July 1798 included Joseph Ellison and John Bolton of Clara, John Goggin of Balleese, Edward Dockerill of Glenealy, Samuel Langrell of Ballynabarney and William Carter of Ballintombay.

Many famous insurgents hailed from Kirikee Mountain, which overlooks the Greenan area, not least the redoubtable Hugh *'Vesty'* Byrne, who was Dwyer's first cousin and right hand man. The executed body of their Kirikee comrade, Captain Patrick Grant, was recovered by his relatives from the sea in January 1800 and given a christian burial in the Seven Churches. The popular Grant was prosecuted in Wicklow Town by Mathew Davis of Ballinanty and Patrick Toole of Greenan, who also gave evidence against William Byrne of Ballymanus. Both were killed by Dwyer's followers in December 1799 who returned to Greenan in April 1800 to shoot informer John Doyle.

Folklore

On the night Allen's factory was destroyed it is recorded that *'the Rathdrum yeomen, burnt Fr. Byrne's house in Greenan Beg and the chapel on the brow of Ballinacor, and several houses. Richard Ubank refused to serve in burning the chapel. Sunday morning the rebels burnt Chritchley's [house at] Ballyboy...Allen's factory was for the manufacture of superfine woollen cloths. The Allen family, who came from the west of England, made a considerable fortune. In the burning, Allen sustained a loss of upwards of 5,000 pounds. His claim for the losses was rejected by the Commissioners, which was very unfortunate for the country and proprietor; thereby upwards of 300 persons were thrown out of employment'.*

Wicklow tradition states that in 1799 *'A lot of wretches were picked up at Greenan and put in training as witnesses whilst Billy Byrne was awaiting his trial in Wicklow Jail, namely;*

Mathew Davis, a farmer's son...afterwards shot. John Toole, Greenan, a labouring man (beaten with stones). Mulligan, a flannel weaver, Cripple Doyle, Greenan, an old man (shot at his door), Dixon, a scullion of Ballymanus (quit the country)...Patrick Grant, a respectable farmer...was arrested and sent to Wicklow Jail principally for the purpose of forcing him to swear against Mr. Billy Byrne, but Mr. Grant would do no such thing even for the saving of his life and accordingly he was hanged, and his body ignominiously cast into the sea'. The popular nationalist ballad *'Billy Byrne of Ballymanus'* queries *'Where are you Mathew Davis, or why don't you come on, To prosecute the prisoner who now lies in Rathdrum?, The devil has him fast chained repenting for his sins, In lakes of fire and brimstone and sulphur to the chin'.*

Site

The lower end of the glacial Glenmalure valley was more densely populated in the eighteenth and nineteenth centuries and the destruction of Greenan factory dealt the local economy a severe blow. Portions of its ruins can be seen in the vicinity of Greenan Bridge. This part of the valley is most easily accessed from the north through nearby Rathdrum or from the south via Ballinaclash where a branch of the R763 from Aughrim veers towards Glenmalure. The steep sided mountain valley is bisected by the Avonbeg River making communication difficult between the north and south banks. There are now more crossing points over the river than in the early 1800s when most were deliberately blocked or destroyed by the insurgents to obstruct the movements of their enemies.

Ballinanty farmhouse, Greenan, dates from the 1750s and was owned by the O'Neil family during the Rebellion era. It is now part of Greenan Farm Museums & Maze and open to the public from May to October. This site has been occupied from Elizabethan times and is very close to the townland of Ballinacor where stands the ruined castle of Wicklow Chieftain Feagh McHugh O'Byrne, victor of the Battle of Glenmalure in 1580. Ballinacor House was built in 1780 by the Kemmis family and in the Rebellion years was the home of State Solicitor Thomas Kemmis. This is close to a field known as *'The Islands'* where the rebel Kavanagh brothers are buried.

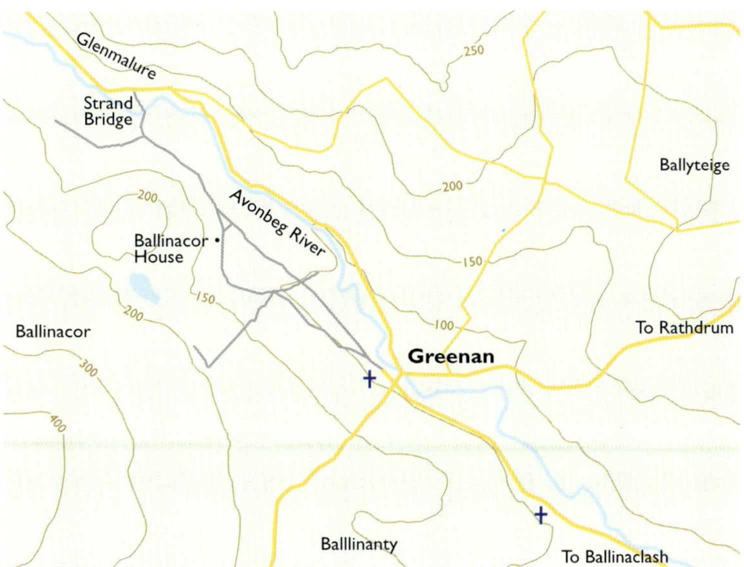

Baravore (Upper Glenmalure) Map ref. T 06 94

History

Upper Glenmalure

The Harney farm at Baravore, at the upper end of the Glenmalure valley, was used as a headquarters on many occasions by prominent United Irishmen. It was there that Joseph Holt assumed supreme command of the Wicklow rebels in mid-July 1798 at which time Glenmalure was the main destination of dispersed survivors of the illfated expedition into Meath. Wounded insurgents and others who had remained in the valley under the protection of Michael Dwyer and Miles Byrne were evacuated to Imaal on 12 and 13 July 1798 when General John Moore's columns entered Glenmalure from several directions. A number of loyalist prisoners were then piked at Baravore where Holt was present on 9 September to receive news of the defeat of French forces in Longford. Phil Harney was transported to Australia for harbouring rebels and his Baravore home was robbed by loyalist extremists in March 1801.

When in Glenmalure the rebels practised drills and manoeuvres which were put to good use in the last days of July 1798 when Moore's troops again descended into the valley. A skillful fighting retreat stalled the soldiers long enough to enable an orderly withdrawal to Imaal. These regular sweeps typically involved the simultaneous marching of troops from Toorboy, Greenan, Rathdrum, Table Mountain and Fananierin. As with other prime camping grounds, however, rapid access was possible to other parts of the mountains where heavily equipped soldiers could not easily follow their fleet quarry.

John Mernagh of Ballinaskea, the *'Ajax of the outlaws'*, became the principal local rebel leader in the aftermath of 1798 and often fought with his close friend Dwyer. On 12 November 1801 Mernagh and his Imaal comrades fought and defeated Rathdrum loyalists who ventured to attend Macreddin's famous annual fair. Such activities contributed towards the decision to locate an army barracks at Drumgoff and the project was one of the five put to tender by the government in February 1803 *'on the line of the new Military Road'*. The road was built over Carriglineen Mountain in the early 1800s from the direction of Laragh and enters Glenmalure at Drumgoff before continuing across the

Avonbeg towards Aghavannagh. It was completed too late to impinge on the United Irishmen, but its imposing presence may have deterred subsequent unrest.

Folklore

According to Wicklow sources, in July 1798 *'The Wexford fugitives and their brave associated men of Wicklow had now to the amount of nearly 400 taken up their quarters [at Three Crosses] in that mountain walled defile Glenmalure. It is situated near the heart of the mountains and the country afforded no provisions unless a few miserable sheep and the most of them were removed from the mountain after the rebels moved towards Meath...But their victorious enemies resolved that they should get no rest there and in a day or two they were attacked by three corps of yeoman cavalry from Hacketstown'.*

'A workman of Malone's of Ballintombay who had just got a protection from General Sir John Moore and the Marquess of Huntley at their camp in Imaal, was returning home across the Black Banks when he was met by the Rathdrum yeomen who knew him well. He presented his protection to them, but they shot him at the end of Matty Harney's house, the uppermost house in Glenmalure. About the same time James Chritchley shot one Timmon, a herd of his own, for some unassigned reason. Of the two latter of these murders there was no more notice taken than if they were mad dogs'.

Rathdrum's Parish Register notes that *'Jack Wayde of Joe Malone's in Ballinabarney was shot by the [Ancient] Britons in Giant's Glen minding his lambs. Billy Manning 'the Briton' of Ballintombay, shot Morgan Toomey in Pierce Harney's land, Baravore, where he was buried, though Morgan had a pass. Two Wexford rebels who were being brought by Langrell and Carter to the camp of the Antrim Militia in Jack Cullen's Parks were shot and buried inside the ditch at Chritchley's, Chritchley looking on. Langrell and Carter were piked the next day at the Orange Stone. Paddy Grant and blind Mick Farrell were at the piking...and Darby Keogh, Ballyshane, was hanged.*

Site

The upper end of Glenmalure is reached by road from Greenan or from the junction of the Military Road as it intersects with the valley and crosses the Avonbeg River at Drumgoff bridge. There is a network of minor roads on the Ballinacor side of the river which permits access to the valley as far as the Strand where there is a footbridge. The Wicklow Way descends to Glenmalure from Glendalough over Mullacor and Ballinafunshoge and spans the Avonbeg at Drumgoff before continuing to Aghavannagh where the rebels often camped in 1798. The ruined foundations of Pierse Harney's house and the adjacent one of his kinsman Matty can still be seen at Baravore, one of the few fordable points of the Avonbeg River where there is now a footbridge. Baravore was guarded by a temporary army camp in the early summer of 1798 which was located in the meadow field known as the *'Camp field'*, just up stream and on the southern side of the ford. Glenmalure terminates nearby at the mountainous ridge spanning Conavalla, Table Mountain,

Camenabologe and Benleagh. Opposite Bendoo, about a third of a kilometre north of the river and midway between Ballinafunshoge and Lugduff, is an opening known as *'the Rebel's Cave'*. It is cut into the steep, wooded slope of the valley where many traces of lead mining dating from the 18th and 19th centuries can be found.

John Mernagh Stone (Ballinaskea)

'Jack Cullen's Parks' was at Drumgoff, close to the Chritchley property at Ballyboy. Overlooking Ballyboy is *'Dwyer's Rock'* where it is thought many rebels were hanged in 1798. The stone is now inscribed with the Irish form of Dwyer's name and that of Feagh McHugh O'Byrne. Although little more than a shell after decades of neglect, the ruined barracks of Drumgoff is one of the best preserved Military Road installations. It fell into disuse after a period of occupation by local miners but retains its original architecture and plan. The barrack structure and its outer walls are dramatically located against a backdrop of Fananierin Mountain when viewed from the vicinity of the Glenmalure Lodge. Troops stationed there would have hindered unauthorised communications with the lower end of the valley as well as the Aghavannagh district.

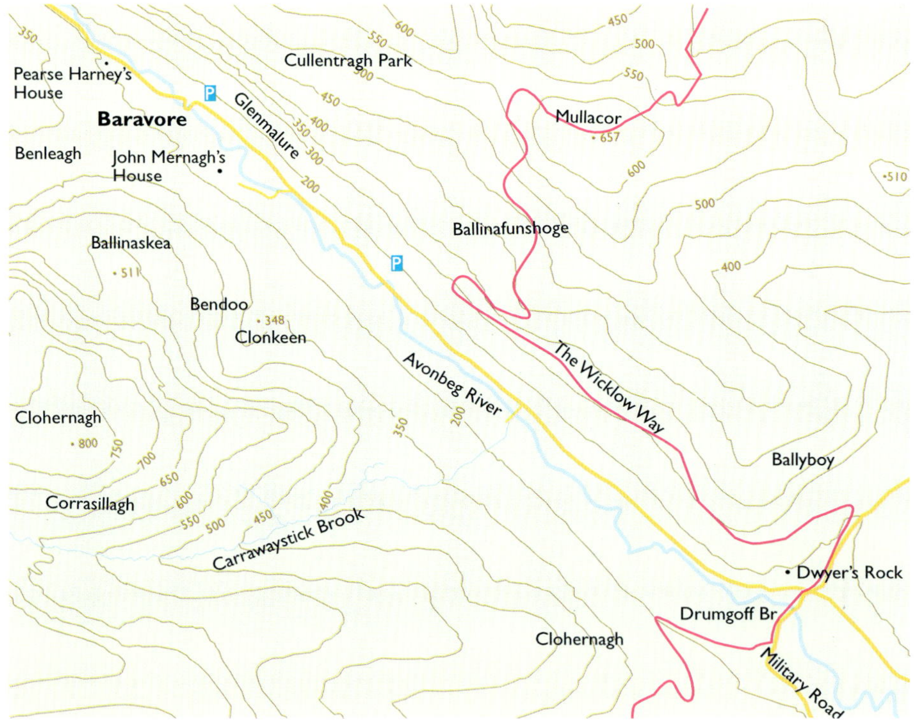

Newtownmountkennedy

Route Five

Newtownmountkennedy *Map ref. O 26 06*

History

The linear market village of Newtownmountkennedy, then the estate of Lord Rossmore (Lieutenant-General Robert Cunningham), was the scene of the largest and bloodiest battle of the north Wicklow Rebellion on 30 May 1798. It was midday on a fine summer's day when over 1,000 United Irishmen from the baronies of Ballinacor North and Newcastle attacked the village from both sides. They had formed up in secluded locations such as Dunran and the Devil's Glen but found it difficult to co-ordinate the attack for maximum effect. A third column expected from the Roundwood district failed to materialise owing to its partial dispersal during skirmishing in their home area on the 29th.

The alerted garrison of Newtownmountkennedy consisted of sixty of the tough Ancient British Light Fencible Dragoons and Antrim Militia, supported by eighty local yeomen. They were forced to burn several buildings to create a protective smoke screen. The defenders lost control of much of the town and became locked in an intense struggle for the market house which they used as a barracks and prison. The coach house stables were fired by the rebels but not before the cavalry mounts were brought to safety and used in the garrison's desperate counterattack.

Englishman Captain John Burganey and nine of his men were killed in the action and many others were severely wounded but the impetus of the attack was broken. Over thirty rebels were believed killed although many more perished in the brutal mopping up operations in which no quarter was shown by the aggrieved loyalists. The inmates of Newtown's guardhouse were also executed. An Orange Lodge was founded in the town during or shortly after the Rebellion and met at Armstrong's Hotel. Most of its membership was probably drawn from the brutal Newtownmountkennedy Cavalry who were suspected of burning Kilmurray's substantial Catholic chapel in August 1799.

Folklore

One of the most popular victims of the murderous rampages undertaken by the Ancient Britons and yeomen on 31 May and 1 June 1798 was thirty-nine year old Michael Neil of Upper Newcastle. After severe maltreatment in the barracks the blinded Neil, a prominent United Irishman who had been dragged to the town by horses, allegedly put his hand on a 28 lb weight *'seized on one of the Britons and beat his brains out. A second rushed to save his comrade, but he sent him reeling to the ground with a blow or two of the same weight. Uproar succeeded consternation. 'Take his life', was the cry. He then hurled the weight with great force into the midst of them, when it struck another of the Britons on the head also...Now [Captain Thomas] Archer ordered him to be dragged out into the street, and a dozen of balls sent through him.'*

The Shorts of Newcastle were well represented in the rebel force which attacked Newtown and were much persecuted in consequence. Owen Short of Keelogue protected a suspected informer on the day of the battle when the insurgents gathered *'up the Ballyhorsey Road, expecting to meet General Holt and his army who had promised to meet them, but failed to do so. The rebels were badly armed as their guns were all seized a short time before the battle, in the garden of Prospect House, to which place they had been removed from Dunran Rath'.* Prospect was owned by one Smith, a yeoman and United Irishman, who had been sworn by John Short of Kilday. Captain Archer of Mount John was told of the Dunran cache and upon finding it empty correctly surmised that Smith had warned his rebel comrades to remove the guns from his garden. John Short was maltreated in the Market House and, after a spell on a Dublin prison hulk, died in Cork Harbour whilst awaiting transportation to Australia.

Site

Newtownmountkennedy is reached by taking the designated exit road from the N11 when travelling south from Dublin. The R765 provides access from Roundwood and the mountains to the west. There is an Irish language plaque dedicated to Michael Neil on Newtown's bridge almost directly opposite the site of the Market House barracks in which

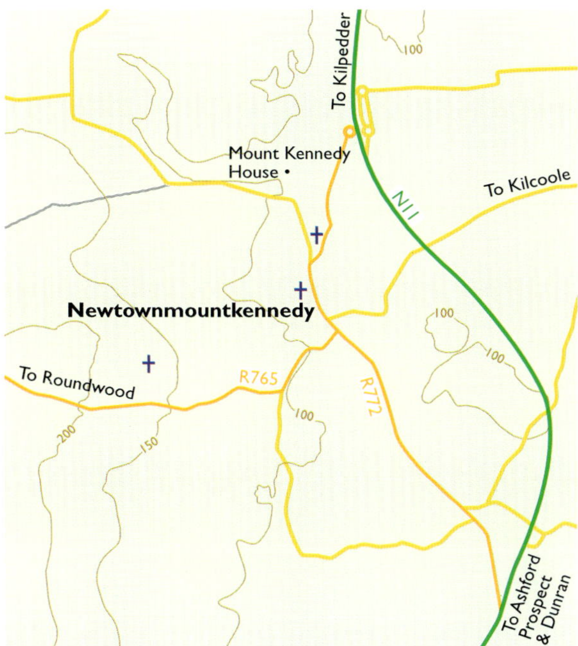

he was fatally injured. His body was recovered by relatives and buried just outside the town at the now disused but cleared Killadreenan cemetery.

The bulk of the rebel dead were interred in a mass grave at Warble Bank gravel pit lying very close to and on the Wicklow side of the Kilcoole road junction. Gravel was drawn from the pit until the 1940s when council workers uncovered human bones. Many crown forces fatalities were buried in the ruins of the now obliterated coach house off the main street while a horizontal slab laid over Burganey's grave at Newcastle's Church of Ireland cemetery is weather worn but legible. The Archer home at Mount John is in good repair south of Killadreenan near Dunran Hill, as is Mount Kennedy House, once owned by Lord Rossmore at the Dublin end of the town.

Roundwood Map ref. O 19 03

History

The townlands around the mountain village of Roundwood witnessed one of the most daring insurgent actions in north Wicklow on the night of 14 June 1798. Rebels attached to Joseph Holt then descended from their camp at Clohoge to attack over twenty loyalist properties. They were keen to exploit the fact that pro-government forces were on the defensive in the mountains in mid-June.

Holt's men moved unchecked through Derrybawn, Laragh, Castlekevin, Annamoe, Tomriland, Diamond Hill, Fairview and Ballinastoe singling out for destruction the homes of magistrates, yeomen and other enemies to the cause of the United Irishmen. Roundwood's Fermanagh Militia garrison was absent when the rebels struck and troops from Rathdrum were the first to respond to the sight of flames in the hills. Fr. Christopher Lowe of Derrylossary was credited with convincing the rebels to desist from their actions and, having thereby demonstrated his influence over them, suffered several assassination attempts and the destruction of his parish church at the hands of loyalists.

The rebels returned to Roundwood on 18 June to seize nine men whom they brought back to the mountains. One prisoner reported that they were *'carried that day to Luggelaw mountain where were assembled before night nearly one hundred rebels arm[e]d with guns, blunderbuss & pikes. They had plenty of meat, no drink, but water, they slept that night in the ditches without shelter'*. Roundwood's main United Irishman, innkeeper James Kavanagh, was then imprisoned in Rathdrum for seditious activities and was credited with initiating the dynamic Holt into the United Irishmen. Kavanagh narrowly avoided transportation but a Roundwood competitor named Fleming was much less fortunate and was shot dead by the military in Imaal. John Smith, for his part, another store owner in the village, was an active loyalist who survived a number of bids to kill him in the early 1800s.

Almost 1,000 troops and Dublin city yeomen under Major-General William Myers passed through Roundwood on 25 June 1798 in search of rebels who had raided the village on several occasions the previous week. It remained very much a borderland settlement for several years and in March 1799 Pat Connor was courtmartialled for an unwise, albeit inebriated, attempt to purchase a bayonet from the guard post. Elements of the Fermanagh and the English Somerset regiment protected Roundwood from the worst depredations of the insurgents.

Folklore

The townland of Castlekevin, south of Roundwood, was the scene of a dramatic incident on 22 December 1800 when three of Michael Dwyer's closest associates were trapped by Rathdrum yeomen in the McDaniel household. They were reputedly *'concealed in a cavity under a clump of turf, in an out house, from whence they rushed out...they fired on Mr [Lieutenant William] Tomlinson and his companion, but without effect, and then with precipitancy ran for the open country which they reached, by reason of the scattered state of the troops...After a time Andrew Thomas was killed and John Byrne taken. John Harman effected a most miraculous escape: being not left alone, he betook himself to a most constant flight directing his course towards the Seven Churches...Harman in his flight threw off all his cloaths'.*

Roundwood

Thomas' head was spiked on Rathdrum's Flannel Hall while Harman and Byrne were ultimately transported to New South Wales with Dwyer on the *Tellicherry* in 1805. A popular Wicklow song was quickly written about the events which includes the verses:

Thomas we may now regret his loss we'll mourn in vain,
we'll plant a willow tree on the field where he was slain,
and on the spot where he was shot whole roses you will see,
the emblem of his manly soul now in felicity.

If the French would invade us and to our aid would come,
we'd plant the tree of liberty in the centre of Rathdrum,
and from the spot his head is up you'd see green flags would fly,
and we'ed erect a stately monument to this hero's memory.

Site

Roundwood is most easily accessed by taking the N11 exit at Kilmacanogue and following the R755 or alternatively from Newtownmountkennedy on the R765. Another route from the Rathfarnham area of the city crosses the mountains on the Military Road as far as Sally Gap junction. From there the R759, which comes from north-west Wicklow, should be followed until it meets the R755 near Roundwood.

While loyalist properties around Roundwood were devastated in 1798 the village itself experienced very little damage. This was perhaps owing to its usefulness to the rebels who frequented the district and also due to the absence of a locally based yeomanry unit whose presence would have necessitated more forthright action. The wooden *'cabin'* dwellings of the *'lower orders'*, however, were obliterated in 1798 by the Powerscourt, Rathdrum and

Newtownmountkennedy yeomanries. Although rebuilt in the aftermath of the Rebellion, they finally disappeared from the mountain landscape during the restructuring of Irish rural society in the mid-1800s.

The most notable addition to Roundwood's hinterland is the Vartry Reservoir which in 1867 flooded lands known to the Wicklow rebels and their adversaries. In May 1998 a plaque was dedicated in Castlekevin to the memory of Andrew Thomas who hailed from Annamoe and was reputedly the natural son of Thomas Hugo senior of Drummin (Glendalough House).

Wicklow Gaol

Wicklow Town *Map ref.* T 31 93

History

For a brief period in June 1798 Wicklow Town was the front line between government forces and the advancing north Wexford rebels. Arklow had been abandoned by its garrison after the insurgent victory at Tubberneering on 4 June and only the ill-appointed outpost of Wicklow Town stood in the path of the United Irishmen. Major Joseph Hardy ordered the semi-mutinous army survivors to entrench outside the town which was already crowded with over 1,000 loyalist refugees from Gorey and Arklow. The civilians camped on the Strand for over a month while the more prosperous took ship to Wales and Liverpool. Accommodation was so scarce in the town by the 8th that the Scottish Dunbarton regiment of fencibles had to be billeted in the Quaker Meeting House.

A company of Reay Highlanders remained in Wicklow on 6 June when Major-General Sir Francis Needham's forces re-occupied Arklow. A firing platform was built around the perimeter of Wicklow Gaol to improve its defences and, while never put to the test, condemned United Irishman Hugh 'Vesty' Byrne and two comrades used a supporting pole to scale the wall in February 1800. Many of those executed had their bodies thrown into the sea as a mark of dishonour, a practice which ceased when local fishermen refused to ply their trade. Deceased inmates were sometimes left where they fell for days during which time a bird of prey reputedly pecked at their corpses.

Wicklow Town 1798 Memorial

Hundreds of Wicklow United Irishmen were tried in the town between March 1799 and 1801, mostly by courts martial but also by the civil assizes which were resumed in the spring of 1800. Perhaps the most prominent defendant was William 'Billy' Byrne of Ballymanus who was sentenced to death for political crimes in July 1799. On 24 September 1799 he was taken from the Gaols' debtors room and marched down through the town under escort to be executed on Gallow's Hill. Napper Tandy, Dublin's famous radical, spent time in the Gaol in February 1802 whilst awaiting deportation to Bordeaux. Tandy then smuggled a message out to Michael Dwyer urging him to keep fighting.

Wicklow Town remained in ferment after the Rebellion owing to a rash of revenge attacks carried out by yeoman extremists. Parish priest Fr. Andrew Toole, whose Wicklow Abbey home was burned by orangemen on 12 July 1799, was found dead on Tighe's Avenue in highly suspicious circumstances the following December. The Abbey was reputedly granted to Fr. Toole by Earl Fitzwilliam in gratitude for medical attention he had received from him when wounded on a European battlefield. More certain is that the atrocity prone Wicklow Cavalry resented this association and burned the town's Catholic chapel in September 1798.

Folklore

The O'Tooles of west Wicklow claimed in the nineteenth century that a *'member of the clan, who was imprisoned in Wicklow Jail awaiting his death, succeeded in making his escape through a sewer that led from the jail to the sea. When he had proceeded half way, imagine his horror when he met with the dead body of a brother rebel, who had got thus far in a similar attempt when nature gave way...O'Toole proved himself equal to the occasion and made his way to the sea in safety. The grandchildren of this bold, hearty rebel are still living near Carnew, in the County Wicklow'.*

News of the death of Billy Byrne was quickly sent to exiled United men in Australia and America. In Wicklow, it was said, *'scarcely had the courtmartial found William Byrne guilty when the country was roused to the highest pitch of indignation. Never since the midnight murder of the famous Feagh McHugh O'Byrne on the 8th May 1597 at Fananeirin did an O'Byrne descend to the grave more universally regretted than William Byrne of Ballymanus. The outlaws whose leading acts were now in great measure confined to deeds of retaliation burned with vengeance and fury. They resolved on the destruction of every one of the whole tribe of informers that they could lay hands on'.*

Site

Wicklow Town is well served by the R750 which diverges from the N11 at Rathnew. Wicklow's Historic Gaol, parts of which date from 1702, was restored and opened to the public by President Mary McAleese in 1998. It contains Ireland's main interpretative centre on the subject of transportation to Australia and has a permanent 1798 exhibition. The Gaol is located just off the market square at the top of the town where the impressive 1798 monument known at the 'Billy Byrne' memorial stands. The foundation stone was laid in 1899 and the finished work contains reliefs of Joseph Holt, Michael Dwyer and William Michael Byrne.

The grounds of Wicklow Abbey where Fr. Toole lived survive opposite the Grand Hotel and are within walking distance of Gallow's Hill outside the town. The Hill is now known as 'Rocky Road'. Wicklow is very close to Glenealy and Ashford where the Tighe mansion at Rossana and Mount Usher gardens retain much of their eighteenth century character.

Arklow

Route Six
Arklow Map ref. T 24 73

History

The strategic port town of Arklow witnessed the largest and bloodiest battle of the Rebellion in Wicklow. The town had a long history of political activism centred on several prosperous Catholic merchant families and their liberal Protestant associates. It was used as a base of operations to extend the United Irishmen into north Wexford in the spring of 1797 and was the main conduit for illegal arms importations from Wales. Many disaffected sons of the *'principal inhabitants'* were induced to surrender themselves to the military prior to the Rebellion and were detained as hostages until 1799.

When the Rebellion commenced Arklow quickly became the only garrison of note standing between the buoyant rebels of north Wexford's huge *'Gorey'* army and the capital. Its abandonment by the retreating military on 4 June created a crisis that was alleviated by the rushing of troops to the town from Wicklow and Loughlinstown camp. An English regiment arrived from Dublin on commandeered carts on the morning of 9 June to occupy hastily prepared defensive positions.

Major-General Sir Francis Needham defended Arklow that day with 1,360 infantry and 164 cavalry supported by six yeomanry units. They faced up to 20,000 rebels who attacked from the direction of the Coolgreany Road, the circuitous Yellow Lane and through the Fishery. Over 1,000 casualties were sustained by the rebels in the second most deadly battle of 1798. The wooden shacks of the Fishery were burned and much of the town destroyed by cannon fire. The well equipped military, although battered and forced to expend almost all their ammunition, managed to hold their positions. The main rebel commanders were Anthony Perry of Inch, William Byrne of Ballymanus, Esmond Kyan of Mount Kyan and Fr. Michael Murphy of Ballycanew. Fr. Murphy arrived late in the battle and was killed by grape shot near Arklow Castle when leading the third pike charge against the Durham and Dunbarton Fencibles.

Father Murphy Memorial

The government victory effectively contained the most formidable state of Rebellion within Wexford's borders and Arklow was used as a major staging post for the recapture of the county in late June. Indeed, General Needham's men mistimed their march from Arklow and Gorey to Enniscorthy on 21 June and consequently left a gap in the military lines which allowed the rebels to escape from Vinegar Hill into Wicklow and Kilkenny.

Folklore

Rev. Edward Bayly of Lamberton (Arklow) rendered himself obnoxious to the United Irishmen by his zealous activities as a magistrate in 1797-8 and they seized the opportunity to burn his undefended home on 9 June 1798. Mary Byrne, a fourteen year old milkmaid, strolled past the smoking ruins of his rectory on the 10th and in later life recalled seeing *'dead bodies [of rebels]. lying on the road and the pigs tearing them like anything, all blood from their mouths and flys [sic]. The bodies were thrown on the sands [at Ferrybank] and the farmers took them for manure until Lord Wicklow stopped it'.*

Rev. Bayly's son Henry fought as a yeoman in the battle and afterwards informed him how the rebels entered the *'Fishery which they immediately set on fire-however they were driven from thence by the Ancient Britons and poor [Captain John Grogan] Knox's [Castletown] corps who charged them out and dashed up the lane after them; poor Knox from his eagerness went too far and getting into our line of shot a six pound ball killed him and two of his men'.*

Site

Arklow is most easily reached by the N11 from Dublin which continues to Gorey in Wexford. The scenic R750 coastal road can also be taken from Wicklow Town and passes through Seabank and Ferrybank into the town.

The long curving main street of Arklow retains the shape and many of the buildings it possessed in 1798. Arklow Castle, in which a firing platform was built in June 1798 to elevate a cannon, remains at the top end of the town fronting the Coolgreany road. The Castle is close to the Fr. Michael Murphy memorial erected on main street in 1903 which is inlaid with reliefs of several high ranking United Irishmen. Across the main street and towards the lower end of the town is a green square and gazebo where the town's Protestant churchyard was once located. Gordon Highlanders were billeted there in June 1798 and hanged dozens of captured rebels on yew trees that grew on the site.

The Fishery is identified with the bridge end of the town from whence many inhabitants evacuated themselves in their boats to Seabank or to British ports. Two hundred fishermen joined Colonel Mathew Doyle of Polahoney in the ranks of the rebel Ballymanus Division. The north side of the bridge is known as Ferrybank where conscripted labourers were forced to bury the bodies of insurgents in slit trenches. Human bones have been recovered from the area as recently as 1997.

In June 1948 President Sean T. Ó Ceallaigh unveiled the Dublin-Wicklowmen Association's plaque to Fr. Murphy outside St. Saviour's church, reputedly on the very spot where he was killed. There is a gravestone in Arklow's Abbey Cemetery to Miles O'Neill, a very senior United Irishman who was detained in 1798. The shop owned by his father, where many seditious conferences were held, is now the P. J. Boland building on Main Street.

Aughrim Bridge

Aughrim Map ref. T 12 79

History

Aughrim was one of the few villages of its size not to field a yeomanry unit in 1798 although many of its inhabitants joined the insurgents forces. The town lay close to the Ballymanus estate of the Byrne family, Wicklow's only Catholic landowning dynasty in the 1790s. At least three of the Byrne brothers, Garret, William and Edward, were leading United Irishmen and their influence was considerable in the Aughrim district. It was no coincidence that the first meeting of the County Committee of United Irishmen took place at nearby Annacurra in late 1797.

Ballymanus House was raided in February 1798 and sacked by Tinahely yeomen on 8 May. This incident was avenged on many occasions with one of the more prominent local victims being the Coates family of Clone whose home was burned on 15/16 June 1798 even though they had aided the fugitive 'Billy' Byrne the previous week. Ammunition was

Anne Devlin Plaque

rushed to Arklow earlier that month from a temporary army camp pitched outside Aughrim at Killaduff. On 23 June 1798 Wicklow and Wexford rebels moving north from Vinegar Hill found the bodies of twenty-seven civilians lying dead on the roadside outside Aughrim. They had been killed by yeomen operating out of Rathdrum and one rebel recalled how *'they met with many revolting sights, particularly in the vicinity of Ballymanus. The village of Aughrim was deserted and numbers of the inhabitants killed'*. The insurgents camped in Ballymanus and attacked Hacketstown two days later.

The rebels returned to the Ballymanus area on the 27th but failed to close with a strong army patrol moving through Aughrim. The town, however, was the scene of a more successful encounter on 19 September 1798 when the rebels in the north-west of the county heard that Thomas King's Rathdrum corps and Hunter Gowan's notorious *'Black Mob'* were in Aughrim and had boasted that they would *'make a sixpenny loaf be sufficient supper for Holt and his men'*. Holt accepted the challenge and skirmishing in Roddenagh Woods preceded the expulsion of the hated yeomen after which the town was occupied overnight and several loyalist homes burned.

Folklore

The minor triumph at Aughrim in September 1798 was known locally as *'the Battle of Rednagh Bridge'* during which, according to family tradition, *'Hunter Gowan was making his escape for his life to get away, and his good horse did take him away or he was shot. The boys gathered around him, and they were afraid to fire at him in the crowd, afraid they'd shoot each other, and he got home to Hollyfort in Wexford across Rednagh Bank, and he never crossed the bounds of Wicklow after, while '98 lasted. The other fellows swum the Derry River (the Derry runs down under the bridge) and they swum the Derry River, and held the muskets over their heads the way they woundn't be injured with water'*.

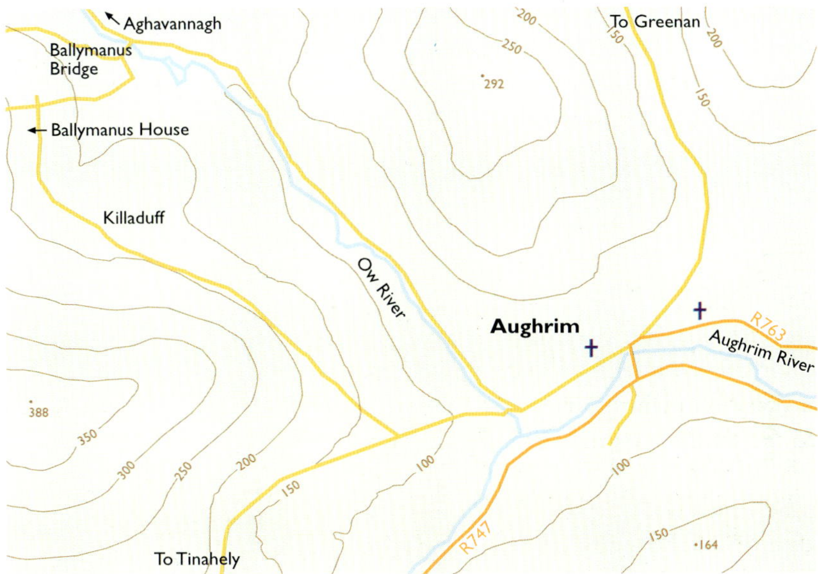

Site

Aughrim is reached from Arklow on the R747 and from the north via Rathdrum on the R763. Another road follows the course of the Ow River towards Aghavannagh, where there is a well preserved Military Road barracks which functioned as a youth hostel until 1998, before climbing towards Rathdangan in the west of the county. Many of the Byrnes are interred in the family vault at Rosahane cemetery. This route exits on the Ballymanus side of Aughrim where the rebuilt home of the Byrnes and an historic plaque can be seen.

It is believed that Holt, whose sister-in-law lived in Aughrim, spent the night of 19 September 1798 in a house of a sympathiser on the main street, reputedly that occupied by Morrissey's shop. The bridge over the Aughrim River has a plaque honouring Anne Devlin who was born near the town at Crone Beg and some years later moved with her family to Corballis outside Rathdrum. The outlying townlands of Clone, Killaduff, Killballyowen, Killacloran and Kilpipe were all scenes of fighting in 1798. Kilpipe was the home place of Daniel Kirwan who was second-in-command of the Ballymanus Division until killed at the Battle of Vinegar Hill alongside Captain Loftus of Annacurra. Ballymanus Gaelic Football Club erected a monument to Billy Byrne at their club house in July 1998 and a substantial memorial was unveiled in Aughrim on 19 September 1998.

Tinahely

Map Ref. T 03 73

History

Mountpleasant 1798 Memorial

Tinahely was one of the principal settlements on the Fitzwilliam estate in 1798 and managed from Malton (Coolattin) by William Wainwright. One of the first orange lodges in Wicklow was founded here in late 1797 drawing its large membership from the village's predominately Church of Ireland residents. When the rebellion crisis loomed the lodge formed the nucleus of the *'True Blues'*, a 150 strong supplementary yeomanry unit led by Captain Henry Moreton. Moreton's brother James captained the Tinahely yeoman infantry and both units were implicated in atrocities.

Two Tinahely men were flogged in the village in early May 1798 with *'the others looking on'* until they revealed the location of hidden weapons and the identities of their leaders. This evidently occasioned the destruction of a shop owned by Edward 'Ned' Byrne of Ballymanus who, along with his brothers Billy and Garret, was a leading United Irishman. Their family seat at Ballymanus was sacked on 8 May 1798 by Tinahely yeomen who later served as far afield as Gorey. They were pulled back to Tullow when an insurgent victory at Tubberneering on 4 June made the south Wicklow border undefendable. They were joined by almost all their Protestant neighbours together with those from Shillelagh, Coolkenna and Carnew. Most unaligned persons had nothing to fear but over a dozen denounced *'orangemen'* were piked by the rebels at Mountpleasant and Kilcavan Hill.

Mountpleasant, south east of Tinahely, became the main camp of south Wicklow rebels in early June and was probed from the village on 17 June by General Loftus' forces. The soldiers were counterattacked and obliged to retreat, abandoning Tinahely and their supplies to the pursuing insurgents. Lord Roden's dragoons and the Humewood yeomanry arrived too late to stem this flight but killed twenty-eight rebels on Rosbane Hill. These losses were avenged by the burning of Tinahely which remained uninhabitable until rebuilt by Earl Fitzwilliam after the Rebellion.

Folklore

Memory of the petty persecutions of the Tinahely orangemen was preserved by Mathew O'Toole of Ballinglen whose brother fought as a rebel officer at the battle of Vinegar Hill. Once, prior to May 1798, O'Toole saw loyalists *'place an Orange flag over the bridge leading to Crossbridge Chapel from Tinahely, to compel the priest and the Catholics to go under it on their way to Mass. The priest refused to do so and instead...rode his horse across the river, although it was a very wet Sunday morning, and a great flood in the river'.* After Mass O'Toole distracted the orangemen long enough for the clergyman to recross in a dignified manner and afterwards joined the Irish Brigade in France.

Tinahely yeomen were proud of their loyal service in 1798 and one recalled how the True Blues and infantry seized one Doyle at Kilpipe churchyard on 27 May 1798 whom they escorted to Carnew for execution. On the same day *'another party from Tinehaly [sic] at Ballinglen, took three men with pikes, who were afterwards shot near the [Protestant] church at Kilcommon...there was not a night after until after the seventeenth of June, that the same loyal people, and the yeomanry and loyalists of Shillelagh and that neighbourhood, by scouring the country, did not meet with more or less armed rebels [but not in great force] going back and forward, whom they dispatched-not many of the loyalists lost their lives'.*

Site

Tinahely is located in a valley cut into the undulating highland countryside of south Wicklow. It is most easily reached from the north and east by the R747 which connects with the N11 outside Arklow and moves southwards to Tinahely via Aughrim and Ballinglen. The road exits the village and follows the course of the Derry river through Cross Bridge and onwards to Hacketstown on the Carlow border.

The devastating impact of the Rebellion has ensured that little of the original village survives although two cannon balls fired by the rebels at Mountpleasant once lodged in the arch of the bridge leading into Tinahely. Others sheared branches from the trees lining the *'Church Lane'*. The traditional market square plan of Tinahely, however, remains very much as it was in 1798 but is notable for its lack of a memorial to the events of that year. The refurbished court house building stands on the site of James Moreton's town house.

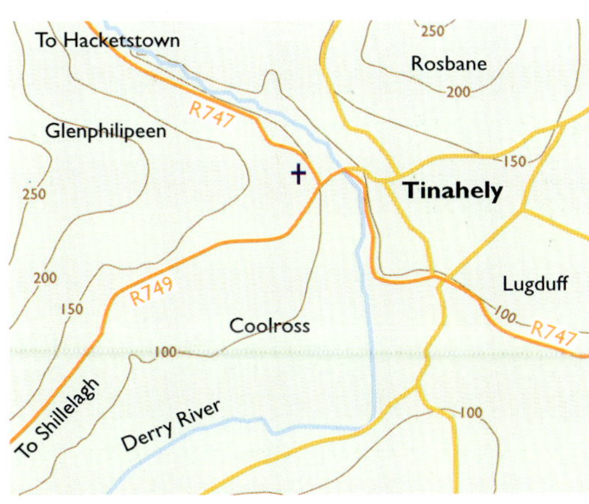

A plaque designed by Patrick Doyle of Coolkenna was unveiled in 1960 on Ballinglen Bridge in honour of executed United Irishmen Patrick and Philip Lacey. Liam Brennan's more substantial *'United in Time'* memorial was dedicated on nearby Mountpleasant on 1 May 1998. Another sizable sculpture was unveiled during the bicentenary at Churchland Crosslands outside Tinahely.

Ballyrahan Hill Map ref. T 01 70

History

Ballyrahan Hill, south of Tinahely on the Shillelagh road, was the location of an intense clash on 2 July 1798 in which nineteen yeomen and several dozen Wicklow rebels were killed. Unlike the nearby heights of Mountpleasant and Kilcavan Hill, Ballyrahan was not used by the rebels as a camp. It was, however, a suitable vantage on which to engage their enemies when they were unexpectedly encountered on 2nd July. The rebels had left Ballymanus estate outside Aughrim and approached the largely destroyed village of Tinahely which they had burned two weeks before. They killed several loyalists on their march who lived on or near the Shillelagh Road, including orangeman William Waters of Cronelea.

Later that day the combined yeomen infantry corps of Coolattin, Tinahely and Coolkenna, supported by the Shillelagh and Wingfield Cavalry, were sighted coming from the direction of Laragh where they had killed several suspected rebels. The insurgents took up firing positions on Ballyrahan and quickly obliged the mounted yeomen and Tinahely Infantry to withdraw. Most of the remainder of the patrol sought refuge in Major Joseph Chamney's fortified mansion on the hill from which they offered stiff resistance to the rebels. Its owner was a well liked moderate and a former officer in the patriotic Rockingham Volunteers of Shillelagh. In 1798 he captained the Coolattin Infantry and died early in the action along with his nephew and the Coolkenna Infantry's Captain Abraham Nixon senior.

The neighbouring residence, Fort-town House, was owned by Tinahely True Blue leader Henry Moreton, and was fired at the first opportunity by the rebels along with Chamney's barn. This proved a costly error as the flames illuminated the attackers to their enemies once darkness fell. Repeated efforts to storm and burn Chamney's came to nought leaving Garret Byrne little option but conserve his forces and pull back to White Heaps on Croghan Mountain for the night. Loyalists claimed that 130 insurgents were killed in the action.

Folklore

When the Coolkenna yeomen fled from Ballyrahan through Stranakelly *'the bullets began to sweep the road and young Nixon's horse was shot under him. He shouted to a mounted yeoman named Wall to take him up on the horse behind him, but Wall said "It is every man for himself today", so Nixon grabbed Wall's stirrup and got safely to the crossroads. Here the yeomen wheeled to the left for Ballynultagh as the high ditch road gave them cover from the bullets which were coming from Ballyraheen Hill...Garret said he would get revenge for the shooting of his brother. He saw Lennon [of Coolkenna] making for where he was [on Ballynultagh] and watching back over his shoulder at dreaded Ballyraheen. Garret brought the heavy fork down on Lennon's skull and killed him'.*

Ballyrahan 1798 Cross

A Tinahely loyalist noted in 1799 that the *'celebrated Bridget Dolan'* tended rebel wounded in a cabin near Ballyrahan on 2 July 1798 and was

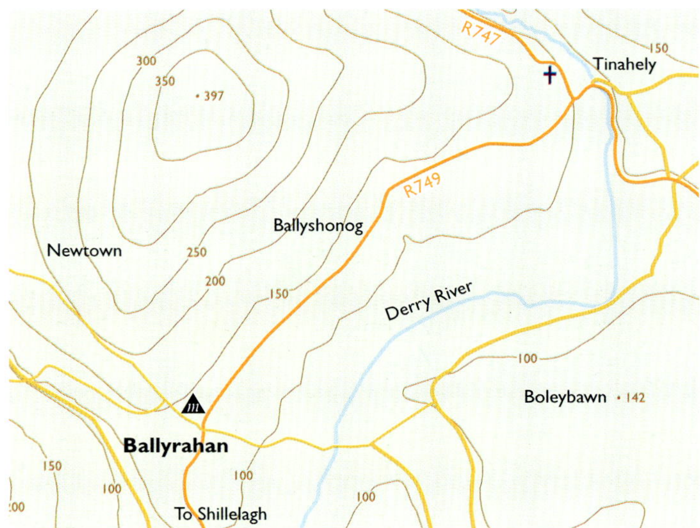

'very active and handy at that business; her story was, that one man had come to that cabin for a coal of fire, and desired that several there might go with him, to see the heretics in Ballyrahine-house made ashes of...in a short time the same man returned: when she asked him what brought him back so soon, he said he was wounded; upon which she desired him to sit down, until the other wounded men were dressed; when preparing to dress him, to her very great surprise, she found him dead, having expired without a groan or sigh'.

Site

The 1798 monument at Ballyrahan crossroads marks the site of the Battle of that name on the route of the R749 from Tinahely to Shillelagh. Most of the fighting occurred on Ballyrahan Hill itself which overlooks the road on the same side of the crossroads as the memorial. The skeletons of two United men were disturbed by a ploughman in 1913 on the site of Ballyrahan school and were reinterred in Mullinacluffe cemetery.

Chamney's death was commemorated by a memorial tablet in Carnew church in 1806 which reads *'Sacred to the memory of Joseph Chamney E[s]qre of Ballyrahin [sic] late Captain of [the] Coolat[t]in Yeomen Infantry in the county of Wicklow [.] on the 2nd day of July 1798 and the 52nd year of his age he was killed with his nephew a most amiable youth both fighting a battle of their God and their king in defence of their religion and their country [.] in testimony of the high sense entertained by his many public and private virtues which are intleliby [sic] graven on the hearts of his numerous and sorrowing friends they have erected this monument Anno Domini 1806'.* His mansion and the rebuilt home of Fort-town House are still features of Ballyrahan Hill.

Carnew Castle

Carnew *Map ref.* T 01 63

History

The political and religious demography of Carnew ensured that it was one of the most volatile flashpoints in 1798. At the same time that disaffected liberal Protestants like John Fowler swore the oath of the United Irishmen, their conservative neighbours rallied around Captain Thomas Swan's Carnew Infantry and the Orange Order. Many rebels lived in nearby Tomacork, Tombreen and Cronyhorn and their arms raiding and arson attacks elicited extreme countermeasures from pro-government opponents. The surprising fact that Tombreen's Catholic Chapel was left unburned may be attributed to its temporary conversion into a cavalry depot.

Rev. Charles Cope was Carnew's principal magistrate and clergyman from 1782-1813, who, along with Henry Moreton and Hunter Gowan of Mount Nebo (Wexford), transported overseas dozens of rebel suspects without trial. On 26 May 1798, just days after the Rebellion had commenced, Carnew's Antrim Militia garrison, Captain Wainwright's Shillelagh Cavalry and local yeomanry corps attacked a rebel camp on Kilthomas Hill. The few prisoners brought back to Carnew were shot the following day along with several local men. This massacre was superseded on 1 June when forty-one men were executed in the ball alley of Carnew Castle.

Carnew was evacuated on 4 June owing to the threat posed by the north Wexford rebels and was reputedly 'burnt to ashes' four days later. Two hundred and sixty houses and shops were destroyed. Ralph Blaney's Malthouse was preserved by the intercession of his United Irish friends and was converted into a barracks once the army returned. The only other building of similar proportions to survive the arsonists was Leonards warehouse. Carnew was attacked again on 30 June by rebels who had just inflicted a heavy defeat on British cavalry at Ballyellis. The cannon-less insurgents could not reduce the fortified Malthouse and incurred numerous casualties in their attempt.

Bridget *'Croppy Biddy'* Dolan returned to Carnew in August 1798 after three months with the rebels and quickly became a state's witness. She helped convict many of her former associates and relatives until 1801 when her reputation was so bad that her services were deemed a liability. Her most notable victim was William Byrne of Ballymanus who was hanged in Wicklow town in September 1799 but at least nine Carnew area men were transported to New South Wales on the *Atlas II* in 1802.

Carnew Castle Wall Plaque

Folklore

Pikemaker James Connors of Tombreen was the first man tied to the flogging triangle in Carnew Castle in May 1798 where, it is said, *'the cords cut in through the skin and flesh and sunk down to the very bone'*. The lashes of the two floggers tore off *'diamond-shaped pieces of living, palpitating flesh'* but Connors would not divulge the location of pike blades he had forged. The untreated wounds quickly festered whereupon *'Martha Graham, a Protestant, a relation of his wife, used to go in and scrape the maggots out of the sores in his back. He escaped by crawling though the sewer that emptied the water-closet, was taken in a quarry on his own land, and again subjected to the same cruel torture'*.

Robert Blaney of Umrygar posted £200 bail so that Connors could visit his sick wife and encouraged him to escape to the insurgent army at

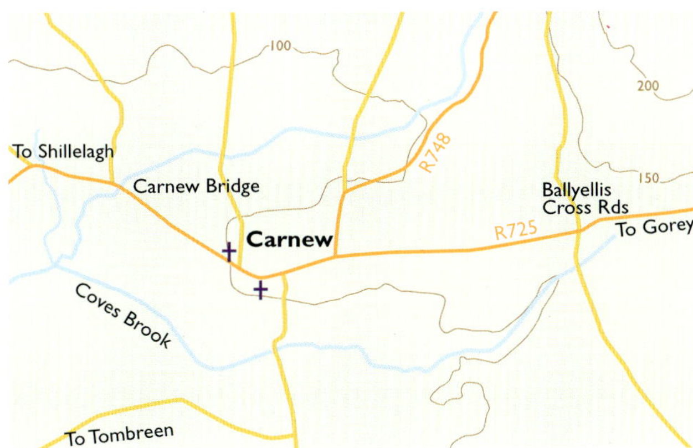

Enniscorthy. When *'all was over'* Connors returned home and *'in the winter nights around his hearthstone would he draw tears from his listeners eyes relating this or some such tale of suffering of our poor people through that awful though glorious year'*.

Site

Late eighteenth century Carnew was the main market town of the heavily planted Shillelagh estate of Earl Fitzwilliam. Despite being twice attacked in 1798 the village boasts two important original buildings. Carnew Castle still dominates the centre of the village and was rebuilt by Earl Fitzwilliam in late 1798 as a residence for Rev. Cope. A plaque inscribed with information on the massacre is affixed to the outer wall which stands opposite and very close to what was once Blaney's Malthouse. The Protestant parish church contains a memorial tablet to William Wainwright.

Carnew is within a mile of Ballyellis crossroads which marks the border with Wexford and is accessed from the Gorey side on the R725. A large stone memorial was dedicated to the United Irishmen at Ballyellis in 1938 and in June 1998 a second was placed in nearby *'Briton's Field'* to mark the spot where the Welsh and English cavalrymen were interred. Their grave mound is clearly visable from the roadside. A third memorial was dedicated during the bicentenary at Tombreen. R725 exits Carnew's main street through Cronyhorn and turns north to Shillelagh. The R747 from Aughrim and Arklow continues south to Carnew which the R748 enters from the north through the spectacular Kilcavan Gap. The R748 connects with the R747 outside Tinahely.

Sources

Route One

Blessington: William Patrickson to Marquis Downshire, 5 June 1798, Public Record Office of Northern Ireland, Downshire MS, D.607/F/196; *Finn's Leinster Journal,* 12 September 1801, Fr. R. Miley to Archbishop John Troy, 4 June 1798, Dublin Diocesan Archives, Troy Correspondence, vol. 2, 116/7/91 and J. F. Maurice (ed.), *Diary of Sir John Moore,* 2 vols (London, 1904), I, pp. 308-9

Blackmore Hill: Captain John Armstrong quoted in R. R. Madden, *The United Irishmen, their lives and times,* 4 vols, 2nd edition (1857-60), II, p. 359

Athdown: *'They [sic] life and adventure of Joseph Holt',* Mitchel Library (Sydney), MS A2024A, p. 58

Oakwood: Thomas Archer, 14 May 1800, National Archives (Dublin), Archer MSS, MS 1017/6/9A-B and Holt MS, p.58

Route Two

Bray: R. R. Madden, *Down and Down in '98* (Dublin, n.d.), p.181

Enniskerry: N.L.I., MS 7665, p.71 and Stephen Gwynn, *Henry Grattan and his times* (Connecticut, 1971), pp. 322-3

Sleamaine/Ballinvalla: Holt MS and Ruán O'Donnell, *The Rebellion in Wicklow 1798* (Dublin, 1998), pp. 243-4

Luggala: Holt MS, p.15 and Information of Joseph Holt, 16 November 1798, N.A., 620/41/39A

Route Three

Dunlavin: Rev. P. L. O'Toole [pseud. Fr. Meagher], *History of the Clan O'Toole (Ui Tuatail)* and *other Leinster septs,* 2 vols. (Dublin, 1890), II, p.517 and W. J. Fitzpatrick, *The Sham Squire and the informers of 1798* (Dublin, 1866), pp.260-1

Baltinglass: Ruán O'Donnell (ed.) *Insurgent Wicklow, 1798, The story as written by Luke Cullen, O.D.C.,* 3rd edition (Bray, 1998), p.74

Derrynamuck: *The memories of William Hanbidge, aged 93, An Autobiography with appendices and chronicles of his family by his daughter Mary Hanbidge* (St. Albans, 1939), pp. 54-5, 84 and 'Anecdotes of Captain Michael Dwyer', *The Celt*, August 1858, p.262

Leitrim: John Finegan (ed.), *Anne Devlin, Patriot and Heroine* (Dublin, 1992), pp. 32-2

Route Four

St. Kevin's Bed (Glendalough): Information of Joseph Thompson, 20 June 1799, Trinity College Dublin, MS G.2.19 and *Dublin Penny Journal,* 8 November 1834, p.151

Rathdrum: Captain John Giffard to Alexander Marsden, 14 June 1798, N.A., 620/38/143; Finegan (ed.), *Anne Devlin,* p.28 and Cullen MS, T.C.D., MS 1472

Greenan (Lower Glenmalure): Cullen, *Insurgent,* 3rd edition, pp.62-3

Baravore (Upper Glenmalure): Cullen, MS 8339, fol. 2, p. 112 and Rathdrum Register cited in Cullen, *Insurgent,* 3rd edition, p. 67

Route Five

Newtownmountkennedy: Cullen, *Insurgent,* 3rd edition, p. 30 and *Wicklow People,* 1939 courtesy of Brian P. White.

Roundwood: Information of Joseph Thompson, 27 June 1798, N.A., 620/38/243; *Finn's Leinster Journal,* 31 December 1800 and "Song on Andrew Thomas" in Ruan O'Donnell and Henry Cairns (eds.) *Ballads and poems of the Wicklow Rebellion, 1798* (Bray, 1998), p. 62

Wicklow Town: O'Toole, *History of the Clan O'Toole,* II, pp. 517-8 and Cullen, *Insurgent,* 3rd edition, p.91

Route Six

Arklow: Murphy Papers, Private Collection, p. 51 and Henry Bayly to Rev. Edward Bayly in Charles Dickson, *The Wexford Rising in 1798: its causes and its course* (Tralee, 1955), p. 256

Aughrim: Holt MS, p. 101 and P. O'Tuathail, 'Wicklow traditions of 1798' in *Bealoideas*, vol. v, no. 2, 1935, p. 162

Tinahely: O'Toole, *History of the Clan O'Toole*, vol. II and John Jones (ed.), *An impartial narrative of the most important engagements which took place between His Majesty's forces and the rebels during the Irish Rebellion, 1798*, part two (Dublin, 1799), pp. 311-4

Ballyrahan Hill: McDonald MS, Private Collection; Jones (ed.), *Impartial Narrative*, p. 319 and Brian J. Cantwell, *Memorials of the dead-S.W. Wicklow*, III, 1975-6, no. 87, Carnew.

Carnew: Rev. P. F. Kavanagh, *A popular history of the Insurrection of 1798*, third edition (Dublin, 1913), pp. 310-11